Essays and Explorations

An English 1 Anthology

Fourth Edition

THE UNIVERSITY OF VERMONT

BEDFORD/ST. MARTIN'S
Boston ◆ New York

Manufactured in the United States of America.

6 5 4 3
f e d c

For information, write: Bedford/St. Martin's, 75 Arlington Street, Boston, MA 02116   (617-399-4000)

ISBN: 978-1-4576-0735-6

Acknowledgments
Acknowledgments and copyrights appear at the back of the book on pages 149–50, which constitute an extension of the copyright page.

Contents

PROJECT 4

EXTENDING THE INQUIRY

PROJECT 5

NARROWING/EXPANDING THE FOCUS

PROJECT 1

Inquiring into Experience

MERI NANA-AMA DANQUAH

Life as an Alien

From the *Washington Post Magazine*

> I only now understand why it is that people lie about their past, why they say
> they are one thing other than the thing they really are, why they invent a self
> that bears no resemblance to who they really are, why anyone would want to
> feel as if he or she belongs to nothing, comes from no one, just fell out of the
> sky, whole.
>
> — Jamaica Kincaid, *My Brother*

I don't know where I came from. When people ask me, I have to stop and
wonder what it is they really want to know about me. Do they want to know
where I was born, where I grew up, where I have lived as an adult, where I live
now? It troubles me to be so scattered, so fragmented, so far removed from a
center. I am all and I am nothing. At the same time. Once, a long time ago,
when I believed that answers were as easy as smiles, someone told me that
home is where the heart is. Perhaps this is true. Love has always been a magnet.
It is half the sky, the raggedy part that needs to be held up and saved. It is a name
as long as history with enough vowels for each of its children to claim. It is the
memory of wearing open-toed shoes in December. Of mango juice running a
straight river from your hand to your elbow.

Love is a plate of steamed white rice and pig's-feet stew. As a child, this
was my favorite meal. I would sit at the dining table, my legs swinging back and
forth, and hum as I scooped the food into my mouth with my hand. I always
ate the rice first, saving the meat in a towering heap on the side for last. After
I had finished the rice, I would wash it down with some water or Coco Rico,
this coconut milk soda my mum used to buy. Then I would greedily dig into
the pile of pork and choose the largest piece. When my teeth had grazed all the
flesh clean off the bone, I would hold it to my lips and suck it dry of its juice. I
would bite down hard until it broke in half and I could touch the marrow with
the tip of my tongue. Right then, right there, I knew my world was complete.

Several years ago, in what I can only assume was a temporary loss of sanity,
I decided to become a vegetarian. Swept into the New Age organic, fat-free
health obsessions of Los Angeles, the city in which I live, I vowed never again
to eat another piece of meat. Not fish, not chicken, and certainly never pork. In
preparation for what I believed would be a permanent change of lifestyle, I
spent the morning of my first meatless day in the produce section of the supermarket stocking up on lettuce and carrots, and at the bookstore buying books
like *Diet for a New America*. Throughout the day, whenever I grew hungry, I

would pull out a carrot stick or rice cake and nibble, often squeezing my lips into a tight purse of dissatisfaction after swallowing. What I really wanted to be eating was fried chicken. It felt strange to not eat meat anymore; nothing I took in seemed to fill me.

"You'll get used to the change," a friend promised. "Pretty soon, the idea of putting that stuff in your body'll turn your stomach." We were at an Indian restaurant celebrating my newfound diet. I pondered what she said, scanned the menu, reading only the selections listed under the heading "Vegetarian," and ordered the sag panir with basmati rice. When my dinner arrived, a gentle nostalgia descended upon me. The food — a creamy stew of chopped spinach — resembled kontumare, a Ghanaian dish I very much enjoy. I was, all at once, swept up by the force of habit — the habit, that is, of moving my head, torso and legs in rhythm to a series of closed-mouth "yums." Except the pot of gold at the end of my culinary rainbow was missing. There was no meat. And that absence left me feeling so cheated out of an integral part of the experience I was having that before returning to my apartment I stopped by an uncle's house and begged the leftover remains of his curried goat dinner.

My attempt to be an herbivore was but one in a long list of attempts I have made to create or try out a new identity. In my 24 years of living in America, I have adapted to all sorts of changes. I have housed many identities inside the one person I presently call myself, a person I know well enough to admit that I don't know at all. Like a chameleon, I am ever-changing, able to blend without detection into the colors and textures of my surroundings, a skill developed out of a need to belong, a longing to be claimed. Once, home was a place, perhaps the only place, where I imagined that I really did belong, where I thought myself whole. That is not so anymore, at least not in the home that I grew up believing was mine. That word, "home," and all it represents has shifted in meaning too many times.

From the age of 6, when I left Ghana and arrived in Washington, D.C., to be with my mother, who had been in the States already for three years, it was quite clear that someday we would return. There was always talk of going back. There were always plans being made, sentences being spoken that began with words like "When I go home . . ." Even after my father joined us, America was still just a place of temporary existence, not home. And in consideration of our imminent departure, assimilation was frowned upon. My parents tried to fan the flames of our culture within me, in hopes that they would grow into a raging fire and burn fully any desire I had to become an American.

English was only spoken in the presence of people who could not communicate in our languages (Ga or Twi). It wasn't as if my parents forbade me to speak English, but if I addressed either of them in English, the response I got was always in Ga. These days my father, now remarried to an American, speaks to me primarily in English, unless I speak to him first in Ga, and even then chances are he will respond in English. My mother still insists upon conversing with me in Ga. When it appeared as though I was losing fluency, she became adamant and uncompromising about this; in her mind, to forget one's mother tongue was to place the final sever in the umbilical cord. I do believe that she was right, but over the years, I have praised and cursed her for this.

Although we didn't speak English in my house, we surely did sing in it. Music was a constant. We listened to reggae, calypso, high life, jazz, and sometimes R&B, especially Motown songs by Smokey Robinson, Marvin Gaye and the Supremes. We also listened to country music — Kenny Rogers and Willie Nelson (which might explain my Jimmie Dale Gilmore and Lyle Lovett collections) — and disco. On weekends, my mother — wrapped like a burrito in a single piece of cloth and wearing traditional thong sandals — would listen to Manu Dibango while she was frying fresh fish or dipping a whole chicken she had just killed in our tiny kitchen into a pot of boiling water so its feathers would come off easily; or my father would sit — without shoes, socks or shirt — in the living room playing Jimmy Cliff and Bob Marley records, his head swaying from side to side, his knees bouncing. Like my mother he, too, was in the company of animals.

On one wall of the living room where he sat and sang was the long, scaly skin of a baby python. On another was the skinned coat of a wildcat, its head plastered in profile against the white wall, with an oval hole where the eye would have been. Not far from the wildcat were two bows; hanging inside the open arc of each one was a tall, slender pouch containing 10 poison-tipped arrows. They were his pride and joy. Sometimes I would beg my father to pull down the arrows and let me touch one. When he did, I would hold it carefully, my small hand trembling as it wrapped itself around the thin stick. After a few minutes, he would take it from me and place it back in its pouch with the other arrows.

I remember asking my father once if he had actually used those very weapons to kill the snake and the wildcat. I imagined that only someone with tremendous strength could do something like that — a warrior. I don't recall whether he said yes or no, but the image of my father holding his big, muscular arm high above his head and darting an arrow straight into the body of an animal became my pride and joy. But, like the pig's-feet stew, it was a pride that I was able to acknowledge and partake in only within the confines of our apartment. Most of the exposure I had to homes outside my own was through my friends who invited me over to play or eat dinner. Yet that was all it took for me to see how vastly different the life I led was from their lives. None of the Americans I knew in the suburbs of Washington had dead animals and deadly "primitive" weapons tacked up on their walls. They had plaques, awards, framed photos of their smiling families. They had pets, animals that were very much alive and very much loved. They bought their food prepackaged in boxes or on cardboard trays. And there were no bare-chested warriors singing of the Zion train, no mothers peeling, slicing, chopping, killing. Taken out of the context of my home, my life — live chickens, reptile and wildcat skins, bows and arrows — became a source of shame and embarrassment for me.

In this way, the split between the me who lived in that apartment and the me who had to learn how to survive outside it was immediate. It had to be. Initially, I suppose, I viewed that split simply as an external divide, straight and pronounced, like the threshold of our front door, marking the point of separation between two distinct realities. On one side was America, on the other was Ghana. And I didn't know how to bring them together, how to make one make sense to, let alone in, the other.

Why do you talk like that? Where are you from? Is that string in your hair? Newness is easy to detect, especially with immigrants. Everything about you is a dead giveaway. And people constantly watch and stare through the scrutinizing lens of curiosity. That was a foreign thing for me, being questioned, being eyed. From top to bottom, the eyes would travel. From top to bottom, taking a silent inventory of the perceived differences: the way I wore my hair wrapped with thread as thick as an undiluted accent, or in small braids intricately woven like a basket atop my head; my clothing, a swirl of bright, festive colors dyed on fabric much too thin for the shivery East Coast climate.

Being black made the transition from Africa to America extremely difficult because it introduced another complex series of boundaries. In a racially divided country, it isn't enough for an immigrant to know how to float in the mainstream. You have to know how to retreat to your margin, where to place your hyphen. You have to know that you are no longer just yourself, you are now an Asian American, a Latin American, an Irish American, or, in my case, a black American. (Only recently has the label become "African American.") At the time of my immigration, the early 1970s, Washington, a predominantly black city, was awash in a wave of Afrocentricity. Dashikis draped brown shoulders, and the black-fisted handle of an Afro pick proudly stuck out of many a back pants pocket. However, despite all the romanticizing and rhetoric about unity and brotherhood, there was a curtain of sheer hostility hanging between black Americans and black Africans.

The black kids I encountered, in and out of school, were the cruelest to me. While other children who were being picked on for whatever trivial or arbitrary reason were called a host of names tailored to their individual inadequacies — Frog Lips, Peanut Head, Four-Eyes, Brace-Face — there was no need to create a name for me. You — you — you African! Go back to Africa! Who I was seemed to be insult enough; where I was from, a horrific place to which one could be banished as a form of punishment.

The white Americans — children and adults — I met attacked me with verbal "kindness," not verbal cruelty. But it was no less hurtful or damaging. Their branding came in the form of adjectives, not nouns — special, exceptional, different, exotic. These words, which flowed so freely from the lips of teachers, parents and fellow students, were intended to excuse me from my race, to cage me like some zoo animal being domesticated; these words, I realized years later, were intended to absolve those white people from their own racism.

I was among the black people to whom many white people were referring when they said, "Some of my best friends . . ." I was complimented for not talking like "them," not acting like "them," not looking like "them" — "them" being black Americans, the only other physical reflections I had of myself besides my family. But, of course, that wasn't acceptance; it was tolerance.

The one place where I found acceptance was in the company of other immigrants. Together, we concentrated on our similarities, not our differences, because our differences were our similarities. Still, I secretly envied the other foreign kids because I believed that their immigrant experience was somehow more authentic than mine. Unlike me, they were not caught in the racial battlefield of black and white, their ethnicity was visible. Mine invariably faded to black. They spoke languages that were identifiable. Everybody's heard of Spanish, Korean, Chinese, even Arabic. The few people who had heard of Ga and Twi colonially labeled them dialects, not languages. Of all the other immigrants, I got along best with my Spanish-speaking friends. For me, they were the middle ground between America and Africa. So when I grew tired of being pendulous, of going to and fro, I entered their culture and it became my home away from home.

In the second grade, I started taking Spanish lessons at my school, and the connection I already felt to that culture was quickly validated. One morning we were learning the Spanish words for breakfast, lunch, dinner, and all the foods usually served during those meals. The teacher, a heavy-hipped Nicaraguan woman with arms that looked like rolling pins, held up a card with a picture of a hazel-colored loaf of bread on it. When she flipped the card over to show us its name in Spanish, the word pan was written there in big, bold letters. My jaw dropped in amazement. Pan also meant bread in Twi.

One by one, I discovered other words, found other sources of affirmation, the biggest being the fact that I had the best of approvals, parental permission, to assimilate into that world. My mum was no stranger to it herself. She did the bulk of her shopping at bodegas, rummaging the shelves for suitable replacements for ingredients needed to prepare customary Ghanaian dishes. Often enough, she would take me along when she went to these stores, where stodgy men in blood-smeared aprons would greet us from behind their butcher blocks with smiles and deep-diaphragmed laughter. I felt a sense of freedom in the narrow aisles of those stores, with the tickling smells of hot peppers and the loud chorus of tongues that were kin to my own. I was both outside and inside the split, the distance between home and here.

But it was not a steady resting place. The Latino kids were also in motion, also trying to reach beyond themselves, searching for their own middle ground. And when I traced the pattern of their movements, it led me right back into my skin. Their middle ground, en route to whiteness — the ultimate immigrant assimilation goal — was black America. So I followed them there. By then, I had befriended two black American siblings, Karen and Allen, who lived with their mother in an apartment upstairs from mine. Allen (who is now married to a Ghanaian woman) and I were the same age, but I was closer to Karen, who was a year older. She taught me how to jump double Dutch and "snap" back when kids teased me.

"Tell 'em, 'Yo' momma,'" she'd advise.

"Your mama," I'd repeat, rolling my eyes and sucking my teeth the same as she had done.

Allen would always barge into Karen's room when she was in the midst of schooling me and poke fun. "You sound like a ole white girl," he'd say. And, at that time, that's the last thing I wanted, to "sound" white. I wanted to sound like Karen and Allen and all the other black kids at school. Every day when I left their place and went back to my apartment, I would stand in front of the bathroom mirror and practice speaking like them. I practiced and practiced until, finally, when I listened to the sound of my voice, I could no longer hear an accent. By then, I was in fourth grade.

When I rid myself of my accent, I suddenly internalized the divide, blurred the lines between continents and allegiances. There was no middle ground anymore, no threshold, no point of distinction between one reality and another. I had strayed so far away from the place I called my home that I could not find my way back. From that point on, every culture I made contact with seeped in to create one fluid geography within me. Yet as much as I imagined that I could claim them all, I still belonged to none of them. I didn't even belong to the one in which my family resided, the one that had once provided me the safety of a home base. As with everywhere else, I became the "other" there, unable to fully expand and unfold the many selves I now had, unable to ever again feel completely whole.

It seems fitting that, of all the cities I could have chosen to live in when I moved from the city where I grew up, I found myself in Los Angeles. This place is the most accurate external portrait of my internal existence. It is a place where everything is subject to change, where even the land is not stable. It is a city of illusions; what you see is not necessarily what is. People come to Los Angeles in search of their future, in spite of their past. Identities and images are created, killed or altered here on a daily basis. Over a hundred languages are spoken; cultures overlap, blend and produce hybrids. There are African American street vendors selling teriyaki burritos, and Mexican cooks in the kitchens of Jamaican restaurants. Far from being idyllic, it is a city at war with itself, a place where xenophobia and self-hatred run rampant. And I have never felt more at peace anywhere else. As the result of a recent incident with my 6-year-old daughter, Korama, I began, for the first time, to accept myself, my history of traversal. I began to create a context for the cross-cultural life that I have led.

For whatever reason, in the course of one of Korama's kindergarten conversations, she let it be known that my favorite television program is "The X-Files." That afternoon when I picked her up from school, she told me about the disclosure. "Oh. Okay, Korama," I said, releasing a slight breath of relief. I was happy to know that she and her friends were now exchanging what I believed was less personal information about their parents. Just a few days before, she had spurted out, in a fountain of giggles, that her classmate's mother wore G-strings; and the day before that I learned of another mother's recent miscarriage.

"Mo-o-m," she whined, "it's not okay. They said you like that show because you're an alien. I tried to tell them that you weren't, but Hugo said I was wrong. He said that you're not from America, and that everyone who's not from here is an alien. Is that true? Are you an alien?" She stared at my head as if antennae would pop out at any time. I wasn't sure how to reply, but with the shrewdness that parenthood teaches you, I tried to figure out a way to answer her question without volunteering too much information that might, ultimately, confuse her. While I was mulling it over, she and I walked side by side in silence. With each step, I felt a distance growing between us. It was a distance much wider than the gap of generations that eventually settles between parents and children. And it was haunting.

For a moment, her stare was as disempowering as those of the American children whom I had encountered as a child, her questions as offensive. I wanted to arm myself against the pain of being reminded that I was "other." I wanted to beg that little girl before me to try, to just try to accept — if not love — me for who I was, the way I was, no matter how different that seemed from the way she was. But I knew I didn't have to, because she already did. "Yes," I finally said to Korama, "I am." I explained to her that in addition to creatures from outer space, the word "alien" was used to refer to human beings from other countries. I expected her to be a bit confused, but she didn't appear to be. She nodded, reached out for my hand as we approached the street we had to cross to get to our apartment, and the distance disappeared.

When I tucked her into bed that evening, she raised the subject again. "Mom, will you always be an alien?" she asked. And, again, I tried to find a straightforward, uncomplicated response, this time to a question I had been trying unsuccessfully to answer for over 20 years. "No," I told her. "Not if I become an American." Up until the second I said that, I had never so much as considered becoming a United States citizen. In the belief that I would one day return to the country of my birth, I had never made a commitment to being in the country where I have spent the better part of my life. I had always thought of naturalization as nothing more than a piece of paper one received after passing a test, a series of questions designed to assess one's technical knowledge of the country and the laws by which it is governed. If that's the case, I could live or die without that slip of paper, that change of nationality. It wouldn't make a difference one way or the other. I have lived my life as an alien, an outsider trying to find a way and a place to fit in. And it is only through that experience that I have come to think of myself not as a citizen of one country or another but, rather, of the entire world.

DAVID SEDARIS

Ashes

From *Naked*

The moment I realized I would be a homosexual for the rest of my life, I forced my brother and sisters to sign a contract swearing they'd never get married. There was a clause allowing them to live with anyone of their choice, just so long as they never made it official.

"What about children?" my sister Gretchen asked, slipping a tab of acid under her tongue. "Can I *not* marry and still have a baby?"

I imagined the child, his fifteen hands batting at the mobile hanging over the crib. "Sure, you can still have kids. Now just pick up your eyebrow pencil and sign on the dotted line."

My fear was that, once married, my sisters would turn their backs on the family, choosing to spend their vacations and holidays with their husbands. One by one they would abandon us until it was just me and my parents, eating our turkey and stuffing off TV trays. It wasn't difficult getting the signatures. The girls in my family didn't play house, they played reformatory. They might one day have a relationship — if it happened, it happened; but they saw no reason to get bent out of shape about it. My father thought otherwise. He saw marriage as their best possible vocation, something they should train for and visualize as a goal. One of my sisters would be stooped before the open refrigerator, dressed in a bathing suit, and my father would weigh her with his eyes. "It looks like you've gained a few pounds," he'd say. "Keep that up and you'll never find a husband." *Find.* He said it as though men were exotic mushrooms growing in the forest and it took a keen eye to spot one.

"Don't listen to him," I'd say. "I think the weight looks good on you. Here, have another bowl of potato chips."

Marriage meant a great deal to our neighbors, and we saw that as another good reason to avoid it. "Well, we finally got Kim married off." This was always said with such a sense of relief, you'd think the Kim in question was not a twenty-year-old girl but the last remaining puppy of an unwanted litter. Our mother couldn't make it to the grocery store and back without having to examine wallet-size photos of someone's dribbling, popeyed grandbaby.

"Now *that's* different," she'd say. "A living baby. All my grandchildren have been ground up for fertilizer or whatever it is they do with the aborted fetuses. It puts them under my feet but keeps them out of my hair, which is just the way I like it. Here's your picture back. You tell that daughter of yours to keep up the good work."

Unlike our father, it pleased her that none of her children had reproduced. She used the fact as part of a routine she delivered on a regular basis. "Six children and none of them are married. I've taken the money we saved on the weddings and am using it to build my daughters a whorehouse."

After living with her boyfriend, Bob, for close to ten years, my sister Lisa nullified our contract when she agreed to marry him. Adding insult to injury, they decided the wedding would take place not at a drive-through chapel in Las Vegas but on a mountaintop in western North Carolina.

"That's nice," my mother said. "Now all I need is a pair of navy blue hiking boots to match my new dress and I'll be all set."

The first time I met my future brother-in-law, he was visiting my parents' home and had his head deep in the oven. I walked into the kitchen and, mistaking him for one of my sisters, grabbed his plump, denim-clad bottom and proceeded to knead it with both hands. He panicked, smacking his head against the oven's crusty ceiling. "Oh, golly," I said, "I'm sorry. I thought you were Lisa."

It was the truth, but for whatever reason, it failed to comfort him. At the time Bob was working as a gravedigger, a career choice that suggested a refreshing lack of ambition. These were not fresh graves, but old ones, slotted for relocation in order to make room for a new highway or shopping center. "How are you going to support my daughter on that?" my father asked.

"Oh, Lou," my mother said, "nobody's asking him to support anyone; they're just sleeping together. Let him be."

We liked Bob because he was both different and unapologetic. "You take a day-old pork chop, stab it with a fork, and soak it in some vinegar and you've got yourself some eatin'," he'd say, fingering the feathery tip of his waist-length braid. Because of his upbringing and countless allergies, Bob's apartment was a testament to order and cleanliness. We figured that someone who carefully shampooed the lining of his work boots might briefly date our sister but would never go so far as to marry her. Lisa couldn't be trained to scoot the food scraps off her soiled sheets, much less shake out the blanket and actually make the bed. I underestimated both his will and his patience. They had lived together for close to three years when I dropped by unannounced and found my sister standing at the sink with a sponge in one hand and a plate in the other. She still hadn't realized the all-important role of detergent, but she was learning. Bob eventually cut his hair and returned to college, abandoning his shovel for a career in corporate real estate. He was a likable guy; it was the marrying part that got to me. "My sister's wedding" was right up there with "my recent colostomy" in terms of three-word phrases I hoped never to use.

Three weeks before the wedding, my mother called to say she had cancer. She'd gone to a doctor complaining about a ringing in her ear, and the resulting tests revealed a substantial tumor in her lung. "They tell me it's the size of a lemon," she said. "Not a tiny fist or an egg, but a lemon. I think they describe it in terms of fruit so as not to scare you, but come on, who wants a lemon in their lung? They're hoping to catch it before it becomes a peach or a grapefruit, but who knows? I sure as hell don't. Twenty-odd tests and they still haven't figured out what's wrong with my ear. I'm just hoping that whatever it is, it isn't much larger than a grape. This cancer, though, I realize it's my own fault. I'm just sorry your father's still around to remind me of that fact every fifteen god-damned seconds."

My sister Amy was with me when my mother called. We passed the phone back and forth across my tiny New York kitchen and then spent the rest of the evening lying in bed, trying to convince each other that our mother would get better but never quite believing it. I'd heard of people who had survived cancer, but most of them claimed to get through it with the aid of whole grains and spiritual publications that encouraged them to sit quietly in a lotus position. They envisioned their tumors and tried to reason with them. Our mother was not the type to greet the dawn or cook with oats and barley. She didn't reason, she threatened; and if that didn't work, she chose to ignore the problem. We couldn't picture her joining a support group or trotting through the mall in a warm-up suit. Sixty-two years old and none of us had ever seen her in a pair of slacks. I'm not certain why, but it seemed to me that a person needed a pair of pants in order to defeat cancer. Just as important, they needed a plan. They needed to accept the idea of a new and different future, free of crowded ashtrays and five-gallon jugs of wine and scotch. They needed to believe that such a life might be worth living. I didn't know that I'd be able to embrace such an unre-warding future, but I hoped that she could. My brother, sisters, and I undertook a campaign to bolster her spirits and suggest new and exciting hobbies she might explore once she was cured and back on her feet.

"It'll be great," I said. "You could, I don't know, maybe you could learn to pilot small planes or volunteer to hold crack babies. There are a lot of things an older person can do with her time rather than smoke and drink."

"Please don't call me stoned on pot and tell me there are lots of things I can do with my life," she said. "I just got off the phone with your brother, who suggested I open up a petting zoo. If that's what being high does for a person, then what I really need to do is start smoking marijuana, which would be a bit difficult for me since the last time I saw my right lung it was lying in the bot-tom of a pan."

In truth, her lungs were right where they'd always been. The cancer was too far advanced and she was too weak to survive an operation. The doctor decided to send her home while he devised a plan. The very word sounded hopeful to us, a plan. "The doctor has a plan!" my sisters and I crowed to one another.

"Right," my mother said. "He plans to golf on Saturday, sail on Sunday, and ask for my eyes, kidneys, and what's left of my liver on that following Mon-day. That's his plan."

We viewed it as a bad sign when she canceled her subscription to *People* magazine and took to buying her cigarettes in packs rather than cartons. She went through her jewelry box, calling my sisters to ask if they preferred pearls or gems. "Right now, the rubies are in a brooch shaped like a candy cane, but you can probably get more money if you have them removed and just sell the stones." In her own way she had already begun to check out, giving up on the plan before it was even announced. *But what about us?* I wanted to say. *Aren't we reason enough to carry on?* I thought of the unrelenting grief we had caused her over the years and answered the question myself. It was her hope to die before one of us landed in jail.

"What's Amy planning on wearing to this little Pepsi commercial," my mother asked, referring to the mountaintop ceremony. "Tell me it's not that wedding dress, please."

Lisa had decided to be married in a simple cream-colored suit, the sort of thing one might wear to work on the day of their employee evaluation. Figuring that at least somebody ought to look the part, Amy had the idea to attend the ceremony dressed in a floor-length wedding gown, complete with veil and train. In the end, she wound up wearing something my mother hated even more, a pink cocktail dress outfitted with detachable leg-o'-mutton sleeves. It wasn't like her to care what anyone wore, but she used the topic to divert attention from what we came to refer to as her "situation." If she'd had it her way, we would never have known about the cancer. It was our father's idea to tell us, and she had fought it, agreeing only when he threatened to tell us himself. Our mother worried that once we found out, we would treat her differently, delicately. We might feel obliged to compliment her cooking and laugh at all her jokes, thinking always of the tumor she was trying so hard to forget. And that is exactly what we did. The knowledge of her illness forced everything into the spotlight and demanded that it be memorable. We were no longer calling our mother. Now we were picking up the telephone to call our mother with cancer. Bad day at work? All you had to do was say, "I'm sorry I forgot to vacuum beneath the cushions of your very lovely, very expensive Empire sofa, Mrs. Walman. I know how much it means to you. I guess I should be thinking of more important things than my mother's inoperable cancer."

We weren't the ones who were sick, but still, the temptation was so great. Here we could get the sympathy without enduring any of the symptoms. And we deserved sympathy, didn't we?

Speaking to our mother, we realized that any conversation might be our last, and because of that, we wanted to say something important. What could one say that hadn't already been printed on millions of greeting cards and helium balloons?

"I love you," I said at the end of one of our late-night phone calls.

"I am going to pretend I didn't hear that," she said. I heard a match strike in the background, the tinkling of ice cubes in a raised glass. And then she hung up. I had never said such a thing to my mother, and if I had it to do over again, I would probably take it back. Nobody ever spoke that way except Lisa. It was queer to say such a thing to someone unless you were trying to talk them out of money or into bed, our mother had taught that when we were no taller than pony kegs. I had known people who said such things to their parents, "I love you," but it always translated to mean "I'd love to get off the phone with you."

We gathered together for the wedding, which took place on a clear, crisp October afternoon. The ceremony was held upon a grassy precipice that afforded magnificent views of the surrounding peaks, their trees resplendent in fiery red and orange. It was easy to imagine, looking out over the horizon, that we were it, the last remaining people on the face of the earth. The others had been wiped out by disease and famine, and we had been chosen to fashion a new and better world. It was a pleasant thought until I pictured us foraging for berries and having to bathe in ice-cold streams. Bob's family, hearty and robust, could probably pull it off, but the rest of us would wither and die shortly after we'd run out of shampoo.

My father wept openly during the ceremony. The rest of us studied his crumpled face and fought hard not to follow his example. What was this emotion? My sister was getting married to a kind and thoughtful man who had seen her through a great many hardships. Together they shared a deep commitment to Mexican food and were responsible card-carrying members of the North American Caged Bird Society. The tacos and parrots were strictly between Lisa and Bob, but the rest of her belonged to us. Standing in a semicircle on top of that mountain, it became clear that while Lisa might take on a different last name, she could never escape the pull of our family. Marriage wouldn't let her off the hook, even if she wanted it to. She could move to Antarctica, setting up house in an underground bunker, but still we would track her down. It was senseless to run. Ignore our letters and phone calls, and we would invade your dreams. I'd spent so many years thinking marriage was the enemy that when the true danger entered our lives, I was caught completely off guard. The ceremony inspired a sense of loss directed not at Lisa, but at our mother.

"No booze?" she moaned. My mother staggered toward the buffet table, its retractable legs trembling beneath the weight of sparkling waters, sausage biscuits, and decaffeinated coffee.

"No booze," Lisa had announced a week before the ceremony. "Bob and I have decided we don't want that kind of a wedding."

"Which kind?" my mother asked. "The happy kind? You and Bob might be thrilled to death, but the rest of us will need some help working up the proper spirit."

She didn't look much different than she had the last time I'd seen her. The chemotherapy had just begun, and she'd lost — at most — maybe five pounds. A casual acquaintance might not have noticed any change at all. We did only because we knew, everyone on that mountaintop knew, that she had cancer. That she was going to die. The ceremony was relatively small, attended by both families and an assortment of Lisa's friends, most of whom we had never met but could easily identify. These were the guests who never once complained about the absence of alcohol.

"I just want you to know that Colleen and I both love your sister Lisa so much," the woman said, her eyes moist with tears. "I know we've never been formally introduced, but would you mind if I gave you a big fat hug?"

With the exception of Lisa, we were not a hugging people. In terms of emotional comfort, it was our belief that no amount of physical contact could match the healing powers of a well-made cocktail.

"Hey, wait a minute. Where's *my* hug?" Colleen asked, rolling up her sleeves and moving in for the kill. I looked over my attacker's shoulder and watched as a woman in floor-length corduroy skirt wrestled my mother into an affectionate headlock.

"I heard what you're going through and I know that you're frightened," the woman said, looking down at the head of thinning gray hair she held clasped between her powerful arms. "You're frightened because you think you're alone."

"I'm frightened," my mother wheezed, "because I'm *not* alone and because you're crushing what's left of my goddamned lungs."

The scariest thing about these people was that they were sober. You could excuse that kind of behavior from someone tanked up on booze, but most of them hadn't taken a drink since the Carter administration. I took my mother's arm and led her to a bench beyond the range of the other guests. The thin mountain air made it difficult for her to breathe, and she moved slowly; pausing every few moments. The families had taken a walk to a nearby glen, and we sat in the shade, eating sausage biscuits and speaking to each other like well-mannered strangers.

"The sausage is good," she said. "It's flavorful but not too greasy."

"Not greasy at all. Still, though, it isn't dry."

"Neither are the biscuits," she said. "They're light and crisp, very buttery."

"Very. These are some very buttery biscuits. They're flaky but not too flaky."

"Not too flaky at all," she said.

We watched the path, awkwardly waiting for someone to release us from the torture of our stiff and meaningless conversation. I'd always been afraid of sick people, and so had my mother. It wasn't that we feared catching their brain aneurysm or accidentally ripping out their IV. I think it was their fortitude that frightened us. Sick people reminded us not of what we had, but of what we lacked. Everything we said sounded petty and insignificant; our complaints paled in the face of theirs, and without our complaints, there was nothing to say. My mother and I had been fine over the telephone, but now, face to face, the rules had changed. If she were to complain, she risked being seen as a sick complainer, the worst kind of all. If I were to do it, I might come off sounding even more selfish than I actually was. This sudden turn of events had robbed us of our common language, leaving us to exchange the same innocuous pleasantries we'd always made fun of. I wanted to stop it and so, I think, did she, but neither of us knew how.

After all the gifts had been opened, we returned to our rooms at the Econolodge, the reservations having been made by my father. We looked out the windows, past the freeway and into the distance, squinting at the charming hotel huddled at the base of other, finer mountains. This would be the last time our family was all together. It's so rare when one knowingly does something for the last time: the last time you take a bath, the last time you have sex or trim your toenails. If you know you'll never do it again, it might be nice to really make a show of it. This would be it as far as my family was concerned, and it ticked me off that our final meeting would take place in such a sorry excuse for a hotel. My father had taken the liberty of ordering nonsmoking rooms, leaving the rest of us to rifle through the Dumpster in search of cans we might use as ashtrays.

"What more do you want out of a hotel?" he shouted, stepping out onto the patio in his underpants. "It's clean, they've got a couple of snack machines in the lobby, the TVs work, and it's near the interstate. Who cares if you don't like the damned wallpaper? You know what your problem is, don't you?"

"We're spoiled," we shouted in unison.

We were not, however, cheap. We would have gladly paid for something better. No one was asking for room service or a heated swimming pool, just for something with a little more character: maybe a motel with an Indian theme or one of the many secluded lodges that as a courtesy posted instructions on how to behave should a bear interrupt your picnic. Traveling with our father meant always having to stay at nationally known motor lodges and take our meals only in fast-food restaurants. "What?" he'd ask. "Are you telling me you'd rather sit down at a table and order food you've never tasted before?"

Well, yes, that was exactly what we wanted. Other people did it all the time, and most of them had lived to talk about it.

"Bullshit," he'd shout. "That's not what you want." When arguing, it was always his tactic to deny the validity of our requests. If you wanted, say, a stack of pancakes, he would tell you not that you couldn't have them but that you never really wanted them in the first place. "I know what I want" was always met with "No you don't."

My mother never shared his enthusiasm for corporate culture, and as a result, they had long since decided to take separate vacations. She usually traveled with her sister, returning from Santa Fe or Martha's Vineyard with a deep tan, while my father tended to fish or golf with friends we had never met.

The night before the wedding, we had gone to a charming lodge and eaten dinner with Bob's parents. The dining room had the feel of someone's home. Upon the walls hung pictures of deceased relatives, and the mantel supported aged trophies and a procession of hand-carved decoys. The night of the wedding, Lisa and Bob having left for their honeymoon, we were left on our own. My sisters, stuffed with sausage, chose to remain in their rooms, so I went with my parents and brother to a chain restaurant located on a brightly lit strip of highway near the outskirts of town. Along the way we passed dozens of more attractive options: steak houses boasting firelit dining rooms and clapboard cottages lit with discreet signs reading HOME COOKING and NONE BETTER!

"What about that place?" my brother said. "I've never tasted squirrel before. Hey, that sounds nice."

"Ha!" my father said. "You won't think it's so nice at three A.M. when you're hunched over the john, crapping out the lining of your stomach."

We couldn't go to any of the curious places, because they might not have a sneeze guard over the salad bar. They might not have clean restrooms or a properly anesthetized staff. A person couldn't take chances with a thing like that. My mother had always been willing to try anything. Had there been an Eskimo restaurant, she would have been happy to crawl into the igloo and eat raw seal with her bare hands, but my father was driving, which meant it was his decision. Having arrived at the restaurant of his choice, he lowered his glasses to examine the menu board. "What can you tell me about your boneless Pick O' the Chix combination platter?" he asked the counter girl, a Cherokee teenager wearing a burnt orange synthetic jumper.

"Well, sir, there isn't much *to* say except that it doesn't got any bones and comes with fries and a half-gallon 'Thirsty Man' soda."

My father shouted as if her dusky complexion had somehow affected her hearing. "But the chicken itself, how is it prepared?"

"I put it on a tray," the girl said.

"Oh, I see," my father said. "That explains it all. Golly, you're a bright one, aren't you? IQ just zooming right off the charts. You put it on a tray, do you? I guess that means the chicken is in no position to put itself on the tray, which tells me that it's probably been killed in some fashion. Am I correct? All right, now we're getting somewhere." This continued until the girl was in tears and we returned empty-handed to the car, my father muttering, "Jesus, did you hear that? She could probably tell you everything you needed to know about trapping a possum, but when it comes to chicken, she 'puts it on a tray.'"

Under normal circumstances my mother would have worked overtime to protect the waitress or counter help, but tonight she was simply too tired. She wanted to go somewhere that served drinks. "The Italian place, let's go there."

My brother and I backed her up, and a short time later we found ourselves seated in a dimly lit restaurant, my father looking up at the waitress to shout, "*Rare*, do you know what that means? It means I want my steak the color of your gums."

"Oh, Lou, give it a rest." My mother filled her wine glass and lit a cigarette.

"What are you doing?" He followed his question with an answer. "You're killing yourself is what you're doing."

My mother lifted her glass in salute. "You got that right, baby."

"I don't believe this. You might as well just put a gun to your head. No, I take that back, you can't blow your brains out because you haven't got any."

"You should have known that when I agreed to marry you," she said.

"Sharon, you haven't got a clue." He shook his head in disgust. "You open your mouth and the crap just flies."

My mother had stopped listening years ago, but it was almost a comfort that my father insisted on business as usual, despite the circumstances. In him, she had found someone whose behavior would never vary. He had made a commitment to make her life miserable, and no amount of sickness or bad fortune would sway him from that task. My last meal with my parents would be no different than the first. Had we been at home, my mother would have fed him at seven and then waited until ten or eleven, at which time she and I would broil steaks. We would have put away several drinks by then, and if by chance the steaks were overcooked, she would throw them to the dog and start all over again. Before moving to New York, I had spent two months in Raleigh, painting one of my father's rental units near the university, and during that time our schedule never varied. Sometimes we'd eat in front of the television, and other nights we would set a place for ourselves at the table. I try recalling a single one of those evenings, wanting to take comfort in the details, but they are lost to me. Even my diary tells me nothing: "Ate steaks with Mom." But which steaks, porterhouse or New York strip? What had we talked about and why hadn't I paid attention?

We returned to the motor lodge, where my parents retired to their room and the rest of us hiked to a nearby cemetery, a once ideal spot that now afforded an excellent view of the newly built Pizza Hut. Over the years our mother had repeatedly voiced her desire to be cremated. We would drive past a small forest fire or observe the pillars of smoke rising from a neighbor's chimney; and she would crush her cigarette, saying, "That's what I want, right there. Do whatever you like with the remains; sprinkle them into the ashtrays of a fine hotel, give them to smart-assed children for Christmas, hand them over to the Catholics to rub into their foreheads, just make sure I'm cremated."

"Oh, Sharon," my father would groan. "You don't know what you want." He'd say it as though he himself had been cremated several times in the past but had finally wised up and accepted burial as the only sensible option.

We laid our Econolodge bedspreads over the dewy grass of the cemetery, smoking joints and trying to imagine a life without our mother. If there was a heaven, we probably shouldn't expect to find her there. Neither did she deserve to roam the fiery tar pits of hell, surrounded for all eternity by the same shitheads who brought us strip malls and theme restaurants. There must exist some middle ground, a place where one was tortured on a daily basis but still allowed a few moments of pleasure, taken wherever one could find it. That place seemed to be Raleigh, North Carolina, so why the big fuss? Why couldn't she just stay where she was and not have cancer? That was always our solution, to go back in time. We discussed it the way others spoke of bone marrow transplants and radiation. We discussed it as though it were a viable option. A time machine, that would solve everything. I could almost see its panel of blinking lights, the control board marked with etched renderings of lumbering dinosaurs and ending with Lisa's wedding. We could turn it back and view our mother as a young girl, befriend her then, before her father's drinking turned her wary and suspicious. See her working in the greeting-card section of the drugstore and warn her not to drop out of school. Her lack of education would make her vulnerable, causing her to overuse the phrase "Well, what do I know" or "I'm just an idiot, but . . ." We could turn it back and see ourselves as babies, our mother stuck out in the country with no driver's license, wondering whom to call should someone swallow another quarter or safety pin. The dial was ours, and she would be at our mercy, just as she had always been, only this time we would pay attention and keep her safe. Ever since arriving at the motor lodge, we'd gone back and forth from one room to another, holding secret meetings and exchanging private bits of information. We hoped that by preparing ourselves for the worst, we might be able to endure the inevitable with some degree of courage or grace.

Anything we forecasted was puny compared to the future that awaited us. You can't brace yourself for famine if you've never known hunger; it is foolish even to try. The most you can do is eat up while you still can, stuffing yourself, shoveling it in with both hands and licking clean the plates, recalling every course in vivid detail. Our mother was back in her room and very much alive, probably watching a detective program on television. Maybe that was her light in the window, her figure stepping out onto the patio to light a cigarette. We told ourselves she probably wanted to be left alone, that's how stoned we were. We'd think of this later, each in our own separate way. I myself tend to dwell on the stupidity of pacing a cemetery while she sat, frightened and alone, staring at the tip of her cigarette and envisioning her self, clearly now, in ashes.

ELLEN ULLMAN

Come In, CQ: The Body on the Wire

From *Wired Women*

There is a male sort of loneliness that adheres in programming. It's nothing like women's loneliness, which might be assuaged by visits and talk and telephone calls, an interrupting sort of interaction that might come anytime: while you're cooking dinner, or dressing, or about to leave the house. Programmer loneliness does not interrupt. The need for concentration forbids it If there must be "talk," it must be of the ordered, my-turn, your-turn variety — asynchronous, sent and stored until the recipient decides to check his email.

There's no substance to this email, of course, no rattle in the doorslot or clatter to the floor. Even responses are rare. Programmers reply by exception: You'll hear soon enough about errors, arguments and disagreements. But all other possible replies — they agree, they don't care, they're homesick, they're not reading mail today — all that is signified by silence. Fifteen years of programming, and I'm used to the silence. I've become accustomed to the small companionships of clicking keys, whirring fans and white noise. Fifteen years of programming, and I've finally learned to take my loneliness like a man.

When I was growing up, the boy next door was a ham radio operator. His name was Eugene. He was fat, went to Bronx High School of Science to study engineering, and sat evenings in the basement of his house beaming a signal off into the atmosphere. The heart of Eugene's world was the radio room: a dim box filled with equipment, all of it furnished with dials and toggles and switches. It was there he spent his Saturday nights, alone in the dark, lit only by small red lights and a flex-arm lamp bent low over his operator's guide.

I grew up in the shadow of Eugene's radio. Over time, his antenna become more and more elaborate, and my family kept giving him permission to add anchors to the roof of our house. From a simple T-bar arrangement, the antenna sprouted new masts and crossbeams, and finally a wide circular thing that could be positioned with a motor. This whole complicated structure whirred when the motor was engaged, vibrated in the wind, was twice reduced to dangling pieces by hurricanes. Mostly, it just sat there and cast an electronic shadow over our house, which is how I came to know everything about Eugene's secret life in the basement.

On Saturday nights, when my parents and sister were out, I could hear Eugene and "see" him on the wire. Perry Como would be singing on the TV set, and then, suddenly, the loud white noise of electronic snow. Through the snow came a pattern like the oscilloscope on *Outer Limits*, which I came to think of as the true physical presence of Eugene, the real Eugene, the one he was meant to be beyond his given body. He always seemed to be broadcasting the same message: "CQ, CQ. Come in, CQ. This is K3URS calling CQ. Come in, CQ." K3URS were his call letters, his license number, his handle. CQ meant anyone. *Come in, CQ*: Anyone out there, anyone at all, if you're there, please respond. To this day, nothing reminds me of engineering loneliness so much as that voice calling CQ through the snow.

Sometimes Eugene actually made contact. Breaking through the television signal came both sides of their "conversation." What they did, it seemed, was compare radios. All those massive structures rising over neighborhoods, all that searching the night sky for another soul on the air, and then they talked about — equipment. One talked — my amp, my mike, over; then the other — my filter, my voltage regulator, over. This "talk" seemed to make them happy. I could hear them laughing: a particularly wide pattern of amplitude, a roiling wave across the screen. If CQ was the representation of loneliness, then this pattern was the look of engineering fulfillment. It reassured the boys in the basement: All that hardware has a purpose, it said. It can indeed bring you company.

Thirty-five years later, I have insomnia, but down the hall my three computers are sleeping. Not sure what I'm looking for, I go wake them up. The Mac PowerBook is really sleeping: Some hours ago, I put it in "sleep mode," and now its small green light is blinking as steadily as a baby's breathing. The portable Sun workstation, Voyager, shows a blank screen. But the touch of a key puts it right back where I left off five hours ago. One small window opens to show a clock. I know the clock is digital, but for some reason, I'm glad it's been given a face, a big hand and a little hand and a secondhand sweep, all of which now say it's 2:05 a.m. PST. The last machine, the PC, is primitive. It doesn't really know how to go to sleep. Like a cranky child, it needed diversions and tactics to be put down for the night: a screen saver that knows when to come on, a human who remembers to hit the right off buttons.

The room is filled with the sound of fans and disk drives spinning to life. Two big 21-inch monitors give off a flickering light. Still, flicker and all, I admit I'm happy. I *like* sitting in a humming room surrounded by fine machinery. I dial up my three Internet accounts one after the other. The net is full of jabber and postings from around the globe. But now I know what I'm looking for, and it's not there. I'd like to find someone still up and working on a program, someone I know — a colleague on my node or one nearby, who'll get my mail virtually "now."

Sometimes I do find someone. Although almost no one answers mail in real time during the day, a kind of license prevails in the middle of the night. "What are you doing on at 2 a.m.?" the colleague writes, finding my mail when the signal he's set on his machine beeps to say there's "incoming." He knows, but here, online at 2 a.m. one does not say *I'm alone, I'm awake, Come in, CQ*. What am I doing on in the middle of the night? I know his workstation has the same small window holding a clock with a face. "Same as you," I reply.

The next morning we see each other at a meeting. We don't mention we've met in the middle of the night. Daytime rules prevail: We're about to have a no-rules battle over a design issue. We can't possibly think about the person who was lonely and looking for company. That life, the one where our insomniac selves met, exists in a separate universe from this one, here in this room, where we're sitting next to each other at a conference table and about to do technical battle. Some implosion may occur, some *Star Trek*–like breach of containment fields may happen, if the two universes meet. No, the persona online must not touch the person at the table. As the meeting starts, I'm distracted. I want to ask him, "How are you? Did you get some rest?" He's inches from me, but in what way am I permitted to *know* him? And which set of us is the more real: the sleepless ones online, or these bodies in the daylight, tired, primed for a mind-fight?

Somehow, in the thirty-five years between Eugene's ham radio and my middle-of-the-night email, the search for electronic companionship has become a sexy idea. I'm not sure how this happened. One year I found myself exchanging messages with a universe of Eugenes, and the next, journalists were calling me up and asking if I would be an informant for a "phenomenological study of email."

This craze for the Internet, it's become a frenzy because of the Web. The pretty point-and-click navigators. The pictures and sound. The Rolling Stones' live broadcast. The Web is turning the net into television — TV for the ostensibly intelligent. It may not be acceptable to say that you have been up all night roaming through the high, weird channels on the cable. But somehow it's fine, impressive even, to say that you clicked around for ten hours on the Web.

The Web has a pretty face. But, underneath the Web is, well, a web. Of FTP sites. IP addresses. Tar files.[1] In this tangle of machinery, email crosses technical boundaries, significant bit orders are properly rearranged, parity bits get adjusted. It's all there to see in the email header.

From jim@janeway.Eng.Neo.COM Thu Apr 27 11:22:45 199
Return-Path: <jim@janeway.Eng.Neo.COM>
Received: from Neo.COM by netcom11.netcom.com (8.6.12/
Netcom) id KAA15536; Thu, 27 Apr 1995 10:55:59 -0700
Received: from Eng.Neo.COM (engmail2.Eng.Neo.COM) by
Neo.COM (komara.Neo.COM)id AA15711; Thu, 27 Apr 95
10:43:37 PDT
Received: from janeway.Eng.Neo.COM (janeway-20.Eng.Neo.COM)
by Eng.Neo.COM (5.x-5.3)id AA29170; Thu, 27 Apr 1995
10:42:06 -0700
Received: from hubris.Eng.Neo.COM by hubris.Eng.Neo.COM (5.0
-SVR4)id AA13690; Thu, 27 Apr 1995 10:42:05 +0800
Received: by hubris.Eng.Neo.COM (5.0-SVR4)id AA10391; Thu, 27

Apr 1995 10:42:04 +0800
From: jim@janeway.Eng.Neo.COM (Jim Marlin)
Message-Id: <9504271742.AA10391@hubris.Eng.Neo.COM>
Subject: Design notes due
To: dev-team@hubris.Eng.Neo.COM
Date: Thu, 27 Apr 1995 10:42:04 -0800 (PDT)
X-Mailer: ELM [version 2.4 PL21]
Content-Type: text
Status: R

This is the true face of the Internet. Most readers don't even look at the header, screening it out like static on a cordless phone. Yet the header holds the real path, machine to machine, the handoff of bits from system to system which takes place under the Web's pretty pictures and sound, under the friendly email windows of America Online and Prodigy. Without the covers, the Internet is still the same old fusty place created by the Department of Defense. And it retains its original motive: a place for the Eugenes of the world to exchange information about, say, rocket valves or caching algorithms. It's where the daily work of engineering takes place, in the famously arcane UNIX operating system, where the shortest possible command is always preferred.[2]

Although few managers would be likely to admit it, an engineer's place in the pecking order is largely determined by an electronic persona who lives in the interlocking email distribution lists called "group aliases." Every engineering project has its group alias — an Internet "address" that sends mail to all members of the team. Names come and go on the alias; people get "attached" and "unattached" with some regularity. Unless you're directly on the node where the alias is defined, or someone makes a point of telling you who's on now, you're never quite sure whom you're addressing.

Often, there are several aliases, names that include ever-widening circles of recipients, from the developers and project leads, to senior managers, to heads of other departments and so on out to the world. It's nearly impossible to know, at any given moment, who exactly is attached. On a recent project, one alias connected programmers and managers from California with managers in New Jersey; after that, other aliases disappeared into more distant time zones in Europe, Japan, India. Once, years ago, I slipped on the "To" line. Using the wrong alias, I inadvertently told a product manager just what I thought of his ideas. My colleagues in the development group — not reading the header, of course, and assuming from the content that we were "alone" — jumped right in with a fine round of character assassination. "Those who can't do become product managers," was the nicest thing said. An alias-slip only needs to happen to you once. Twice would be suicide.

For an engineer, gaining comfort and skill in using these various aliases — and creating the right online persona for each — is a prerequisite for surviving in the profession. Everything happens there: design, technical argument, news, professional visibility; in short, one's working life. Someone who can't survive by email has to find another way to earn a living. If an engineer begins to insist on too many meetings or too many phone calls (womanish, interrupting sort of interactions), he or she will soon be seen as a nuisance and a "bad programmer." Early in an engineer's life, one learns to send mail.

Life in the group alias is not an especially friendly place. Being on the project distribution list is akin to being the object of a Communist criticism/ self-criticism session. Your colleagues have learned to exert technical influence by ferociously attacking your work while vehemently defending their own. It is a place purposely constructed to be a shooting gallery without apologies. What occurs there is a technical battle fought in the arena of technology — a tightening circle of machine reference. In a McLuhanesque way, cyberspace carries its own message back to the engineer: We are mind and machine mediated through mind and machine. A typical posting: "You are running in tautologies. Your whole way of thinking is a tautology. Or else you are stupid."

In this online battle, there is no sight of the victim's defensive posture, of course, no expression of fear and dismay; the wire gives off no smell of a human under attack. The object of attack must tough it out or quit. The sight of virtual blood on the screen is like running from a grizzly: It only makes the bear want to chase you. As one project leader put it, "We try to encourage arrogance."

The only recourse is humor. It is acceptable to designate oneself "the goat of the week." It is fine to say something like: "I agree to hold goatship for seven days, or until someone else commits an error of greater or equal stupidity, whichever comes first." But, under no circumstances, may anyone ask for compassion. For such sentiments, you must go to personal email, point-to-point, perhaps some middle-of-the-night search for company which must be refuted by day. No, you can't ask anyone to back off. The group alias is no place to look for love.

Is it any wonder then that engineers look for company on the net? While most of the world would think of Usenet conferences and Web pages as a degraded form of human communication (compared to, say, a dinner party or even a business phone call), for the average engineer the Internet represents an improvement on daily life in the group alias. The wider net — the conferences, the Web — offer release from the anxiety and claustrophobia of group email. They are places to find anonymity if one chooses, to be stupid (or arrogant) without consequence in "real" life. Travel to far-off places. Have fascinating discussions with erudite scientists around the world. Unburden yourself to a stranger. "Talk" without ever being interrupted. All this and more awaits the visitor to the wider net.

It has taken me a long time to understand why most women engineers I've known did not often fight their technical battles through the group alias (and why we therefore did not need the counterbalance of Internet conferences). We knew it was simply easier to walk down the hall to someone's office, close the door and have a talk. We "codeswitched" — changed modes of communication — as we found it necessary. We might take someone out to lunch, arrange a meeting, drop in for a chat or use the alias. Not all women can codeswitch — I've known some who never left their office; one bragged she had no interest whatsoever in physical existence and, as evidence, told us her home was not permitted to contain a single decorative object. But, being women as well as engineers, most of us can communicate on multiple channels. We use the Internet as a tool, like the phone or the fax, a way to transmit news and make appointments. For women, online messages constitute one means of communication among many, one type of relationship among many. Maybe this is why there are fewer of us online: We already have company. For the men, their online messages *are* their relationships. They seem content in the net's single channeledness, relations wrapped in the envelope of technology: one man, one wire.

There is, therefore, a usual gender-role reversal in the way men and women use the Internet. Men net-surf the way suburban women of the 1950s and 1960s used the telephone: as a way to break out of isolation. For nothing in today's world so much resembles the original suburbia as the modern software-engineering campus.

Close by a freeway on-ramp, meticulously planned and laid out, the engineering campus is nothing if not a physical and mental Levittown. It is endowed with artificial nature — bushes and hedges to soften the lines of parking lots. It reassures its inhabitants with splashing fountains, faux waterfalls, and fake lagoons where actual ducks sometimes take up residence. And there are those regular rows of offices: ranch houses for the intellect. Better ones overlook the lagoons; lesser ones, the parking lot. But, aside from small differences in size and orientation, the "houses" are all alike. The occupants are supposed to be comforted by the computerized equivalent of the washer-dryer and all-electric kitchen: workstations, network connections, teleconferencing cameras — *appliances.*

There, in this presumed paradise, engineers are stranded in the company of an infantile mentality: the machine. The computer, as the engineer sees it, makes a toddler seem brilliant. For what engineers do is create artificial smartness. Our job is to make a simulacrum of intelligence, a thing that seems to contain knowledge only because it has been programmed to behave that way. We are the ones who create the pretty pictures and sound; we make the point-and-click interfaces. But the thing we talk to all day may be little more than a mechanism that reads bits off a disk drive. It does not "understand" us. If a comma is out of place, it complains like a toddler who won't tolerate a pea touching the mashed potatoes. And, exhausted though the programmer may be, the machine is like an uncanny child that never gets tired. This is the general definition of the modern software engineer: a man left alone all day with a cranky, illiterate thing, which he must somehow make grow up. It is an odd gender revenge.

Is it any surprise that these isolated men need relief, seek company, hook up to the net? Cyberspace: the latest form of phone yakking. Internet: mother's little helper for the male engineer.

This is not to say that women are not capable of engineering's malelike isolation. Until I became a programmer, I didn't thoroughly understand the usefulness of such isolation: the silence, the reduction of life to thought and form; for example, going off to a dark room to work on a program when relations with people get difficult. I'm perfectly capable of this isolation. I first noticed it during the visit of a particularly tiresome guest. All I could think was, there's that bug waiting for me, I really should go find that bug.

Women are supposed to prefer talking. I've been told that women have trouble as engineers because we'd rather relate to people than to machines. This is a thorough misconception. The fact that I can talk to people in no way obviates my desire (yes, *desire*) to handle a fine machine. I drive a fast car with a big engine. An old Leica camera — miracle of graceful glass and velvety metal — sits in my palm as if attached, part of me. I tried piloting a plane just to touch it: Taking the yoke into my hands and banking into a turn gave me the indescribable pleasure of holding a powerful machine while *it* held me. I'm an engineer for the same reason anyone is an engineer: a certain love for the intricate lives of things, a belief in a functional definition of reality. I do believe that the operational definition of a thing — how it *works* — is its most eloquent self-expression.

Ironically, those of us who most believe in physical, operational eloquence are the very ones most cut off from the body. To build the working thing that is a program, we perform "labor" that is sedentary to the point of near immobility, and we must give ourselves up almost entirely to language. Believers in the functional, nonverbal worth of things, we live in a world where waving one's arms accomplishes nothing, and where we must write, write, write in odd programming languages and email. Software engineering is an oxymoron: We are engineers, but we don't build anything in the physical sense of the word. We think. We type. It's all grammar.[3]

Cut off from real working things, we construct a substitute object: the program. We treat it as if it could be specified like machinery and assembled out of standard parts.[4] We say we "engineered" it; when we put the pieces of code together, we call it "a build." And, cut off from the real body, we construct a substitute body: ourselves online. We treat it as if it were our actual self, our real life. Over time, it does indeed become our life.

I fell in love by email. It was as intense as any other falling in love — no, more so. For this love happened in my substitute body, the one online, a body that stays up later, is more playful, more inclined to games of innuendo — all the stuff of romantic love.

I must stress from the outset there was nothing in this online attraction of "sexual harassment" or "environments hostile to women." Neither was it some anonymous, fetishistic Internet encounter. We knew each other. We'd worked on the same project off and on for years. But it was a project that took place almost entirely via Internet. Even the software was distributed through FTP sites; we "knew" our customers by their Internet addresses. I was separated from the development team by some fifty miles of crowded freeway, and I saw actual human beings perhaps once every two months. If I were going to fall in love on this project, there was no choice: It would have to be by email.

I'll call the object of my affections "him" or "Karl," but these are only disguises. I'll describe coastlines and places that sound like San Francisco, but such descriptions may or may not be accurate. The only thing you can know for sure is that something like this did indeed happen, and that the "I" in the story is I, myself, contractor on the project.

The relationship began after a particularly vicious online battle. The thread went on for weeks, and the mail became progressively more bitter, heedless of feelings, sarcastic. My work was the object of scorn. I say "my work," but the team made no nice distinction between "me" and "my work." One wrote, "Wrong, wrong, wrong, wrong! Completely dumb!" Said another, "What's the objective? Just to produce some piece of shit to satisfy the contract?" If I hadn't been working around people like this for years, I surely would have quit. As it was, I said to myself, "Whoa. Remember they treat each other this way. It's just the far end of the scale on arrogance."

After I had been run through the gauntlet, Karl did this amazing thing: He posted to the group alias a story about the time he made a cut-and-paste error and therefore became "the official project whipping boy." He described how it felt to be the object of ridicule, and ended with the report of yet another stupid mistake he had just made. I watched this posting roll up my screen in amazement. In all my experience, no male engineer had ever posted such a letter to his colleagues.

To the group alias, I sent the following reply:

Thank you, Karl, for sharing the whipping energies with me. Your company at the post was much appreciated.

Even as I typed a period at the beginning of a clear line and hit the Return key — sending this mail off to the entire project group — I was aware of a faint whiff of exhibitionism. His reply only enhanced the thrill:

Delighted. Anytime.

Then we abandoned the group alias.

What followed were months of email that rode back and forth between us with increasing speed. Once a day, twice a day, hourly. It got so I had to set a clock to force myself to work uninterruptedly for an hour then — ring! — my reward was to check my mail. We described our lives, interests, favorite writers, past work projects and, finally, past lovers. Once we got to lovers, the deed was done. It was inevitable that we would have to go out, *see* each other. Yet we delayed. We wanted to stay where we were: in the overwhelming sensation of words, machine, imagination.

It's tempting to think of these email exchanges as just another epistolary romance — *The Sorrows of Young Werther* with phone lines. But the "mail" in electronic mail is just a linguistic artifact. Lasers can be described in terms of candle power, but there's no flicker, no slow hot drop of wax in laser light; and there's not much "mail" left in email. I have in my desk drawer a piece of paper on which Karl has written the title and author of a book. Here is his writing: precise and printlike, standing straight upward, as lean and spare as his body. Having this piece of paper, I know what the email lacks: the evidence of his flesh, the work of his *hand*.

And, although we seem to be delaying, prolonging the time of imagination, the email is rushing us. I read a message. The prompt then sits there, the cursor blinking. It's all waiting for me to type "r" for "reply." The whole system is designed for it, is pressing me, is sitting there pulsing, insisting, *Reply. Reply right now.* Before I know it, I've done it: I've typed "r." Immediately, the screen clears, a heading appears, "From:" my Internet address, "To:" Karl's address, "Re:" Karl's subject. And now I reply. Even though I meant to hold the message a while, even though I wanted to treat it as if it were indeed a letter — something to hold in my hand, read again, mull over — although my desire is to wait, I find it hard to resist that voice of the software urging, *Reply, reply now.*

There's a text editor available. I can fix mistakes, rethink a bit here and there. But there'll be no evidence of my changes, which makes edited email appear rather studied and, well, edited. No, the system wants a quick reply, and, according to some unspoken protocol, no one wants to look as if he or she had actually spent much time composing. So the ironic effect of the text editor is to discourage anyone from using it. It's best if the reply has the look of something fired off, full of spelling errors and typos. Dash it off, come to the beginning of a clean line, type a period, hit the Return key, and it's gone: done, replied to.

What's missing now is geography. There's no delightful time of imagination as my letter crosses mountains and oceans. In the world of paper mail, now is when I should be hearing my own words in my lover's mind, envisioning the receipt of the envelope, the feeling at seeing the return address, the opening, the reading. But my email is already there. And my lover has the same pressures to type "r" as I did. Before I know it, it's back. "Re:" the same subject. Even though we're both done with the subject and haven't mentioned it for weeks, the subject heading lingers, back and forth, marker of where this thread of messages began.

Still, Karl and I do manage to forge a relationship out of this environment designed for information exchange. He meticulously types out passages from Borges, which we only admire, never analyze. We share a passion about punctuation. He sends me his dreams. I send him pieces of articles I'm working on. An electronic couple, a "we," begins to evolve: "We think that way," he writes once; "You and I feel that way," he says later. Suddenly, we change our signatures. He ends his messages with —K, I respond as —E, like adulterous co-re-spondents who fear discovery.

But soon we come to the first communications problem of our relation-ship: interpolation. The email software we are using allows the recipient to copy the contents of the received message into the reply. At the beginning of an empty line, the recipient enters "~m" and the machine answers, "interpolat-ing message number *nnn*." The result is something like the following:

> There's something in this team's working process that's really broken. [I write in the original message]

I couldn't agree more. [Karl interpolates his reply]

> > I think it's because they evaluate the messenger, not the ideas. I mean, when someone makes a suggestion, the immediate reaction is not to consider the idea but to decide if the person is worthy to be commenting on their work.

Interesting. I've felt alienated for a long time, but perhaps it takes an outsider to see exactly what's making us such a dysfunctional group.

> I've never seen such a ruthless development team.

It's the sort of thing that makes me wonder what I'm doing in the profession.

At first it seems like an attentive gesture — he is responding to my every line — but soon I feel as though I am living with an echo. Not only do I get a response back in a hurry, but what I get back are *my own words*. I would rather see what he remembered of my mail. I would like to know the flow of his mind, how it leaps from one paragraph to the next. But instead I get interpolations. I don't feel answered; I feel commented upon. I get irritated, should say some-thing, as one should in any relationship. But I let it go, just break a thread (I don't type "r," dropping his subject on the "Re:" line) to signal my displeasure.

Months go by. Slowly, without ever talking about it, we work out the interpolation problem. We get good at it, use it. I write to thank him for recom-mending a book, and he interpolates his reply:

> Thanks again for the book. I don't want to finish it.

My pleasure.

> > I like having it by my bedside.

My pleasure.

> > —E

— K

Meanwhile, our daylight life moves in a separate, parallel track. When we "speak" in the group alias, it's without overtones. I even report a bug in Karl's code as I would in anyone's. When I have to write to him directly about some work matter, I always "CC" the lead engineer. The "CC" is the signal: Watch out, pretend you know nothing.

Only once does our private world intersect with our work. I have to get a technical particular from Karl; mail would be too slow, I use the phone. I say my name, and our voices drop to a soft low lone. I am talking about a program — "So it becomes 'root' then calls 'setuid' to get read/write/execute permissions on the file" — but I am murmuring. In my mouth, "root" and "call" and "permissions" become honeyed words. He responds slowly. "Yes. That's what it does." Pause. Low talk: "All permissions. Yes."

Exquisite as delay has been, we can't put off meeting indefinitely. The email subject heading for the past month has been "Dinner?" and we both know we can't keep writing messages under this topic and never actually have dinner. Perhaps it's simply the way words have power over our software-engineered lives: The dinner date sits there as a mail header, and we have no choice but to fulfill it. There are real and good reasons we should resist the header, why we should stay where we are and just send mail. We work together. We're both just out of long-term relationships (which we've discussed). I've tended to prefer women (which he doesn't know; I'm not even sure what I should be telling myself about all this). Still, there is a momentum by now, a critical mass of declared "we-ness" that is hurtling us towards each other. It must be done: We will have dinner.

By the time he is to arrive, my body is nearly numb. Part by body part turns off as the time for his actual presence comes nearer. He calls. He's going to be late — bug in a program, traffic. I hear the fear in his voice. It's the same fear as mine: We will have to speak. We will have to know when to talk and when to listen. Panic. We have no practice in this. All we know is we must type "r" and reply, reply right now. Without the press of the system, how will we find the auditory, physical rhythm of speech?

We should not have worried. We sit down in the restaurant, and our "conversation" has an all too familiar feel. One talks, stops; then the other replies, stops. An hour later, we are still in this rhythm. With a shock, I realize that we have finally gone out to dinner only to *exchange email*. I can almost see the subject headings flying back and forth. I can even see the interpolations: "About what you said about. . . ." His face is the one of my imaginings, the same serious attention, deep voice, earnest manner with an occasional smile or tease. But, in some odd way, it's as if his face is not there at all, it has so little effect on the flow of "talk." I look at our hands lying near each other's on the table: They might as well be typing.

We close the restaurant — they have to vacuum around us. It's nearly midnight on a Tuesday, and he gives off the cues of a man who has no interest in going home. He says "Yes, the beach" before I can even get to the alternatives of the Marina, the new pier at the Embarcadero, a South of Market club. Yes, the beach.

A storm is coming in off the Pacific. The air is almost palpable, about to burst with rain. The wind has whipped up the ocean, and breakers are glowing far out from the beach. The world is conspiring around us. All things physical insist we pay attention. The steady rush of the ocean. The damp sand, the tide coming in to make us scuttle up from the advancing edge. The sandpipers busy at the uncovered sand. The smell of salt, of air that has traveled across the water all the way from Japan. The feel of continent's end, a gritty beach at the far edge of a western city.

Yet we talk, talk, talk. My turn, over; your turn. He walks, briskly, never adjusting his pace to mine, and he talks, talks, talks. Finally, I can't stand it. I just stop. I put my hands in my pockets, face the ocean, and watch the waves setting up in the dark. I feel my whole body saying, "Touch me. Put your arm around me. Only brush my shoulder. Even just stand next to me, your hands in your pockets, but our jacket sleeves grazing each other."

Still we march up and down the beach. He clearly doesn't want to leave. He wants to stay, talk, walk at that relentless, never-adjusting pace. Which should I believe: his staying with me at midnight on a deserted stormy beach or this body-absent talk?

Across the road from the beach is an old windmill that doesn't turn, a *folie* of the 1890s. Naturally he is interested, he wants to go there, walk, see everything. I tell him I think it once worked, something about an acquifer under the park and the windmill used to pump up water. We think it over. It's consoling, this engineer talk, this artifact of a thing that once did actually useful labor, handiwork of the Progressive Era, great age of engineering.

Surrounding the windmill are tulips, white, and a bench. I want to sit quietly on the bench, let my eyes adjust to the dark until the tulips glow like breakers. I imagine us sitting there, silent, in the lee of a windmill that doesn't turn in the wind.

But I look up to the top of the windmill, and I can't help myself.

"A dish!" I exclaim. What appears to be a small satellite dish is perched in the spokes of the mill.

He looks up. "Signal repeater," he says.

"Not a dish?"

"No, signal repeater."

It is kind of small for a dish. He's probably right. "I wonder what signal it's repeating," I say.

We're finally quiet for a moment. We look up and wonder over the signal being repeated from somewhere to somewhere across the ocean.

"Navigation aid?" I hazard. "Marine weather?"

"Depends," he says. "You know, signal strength, receiving station location."

I think: antennas, receiving stations. Spectre of hardware. World of Eugenes. Bits and protocols on air and wire. Machines humming alone all night in the dark. "Yeah," I say, remembering the feel of CQ through electric snow, giving up on the evening, "signal strength."

Near dawn, I'm awakened by the sound of drenching rain. The storm has come in. My cat is cold, scratches at the top sheet for me to let her in. We fall back to sleep like litter mates.

For a few hours the next morning, I let myself feel the disappointment. Then, before noon, the email resumes.

He writes. His subject heading is "Thank you!" He thanks me for the "lovely, wonderful" evening. He says he read the article I gave him before going to bed. He wanted to call me in the morning but didn't get to sleep until 2 a.m. He woke up late, he says, rushed from meeting to meeting. I write back to thank him. I say that, when we walked on the beach, I could smell and feel the storm heading for us across the Pacific. How, when the rain's ruckus awakened me in the night, I didn't mind; how I fell back to sleep thinking to the rain, I was expecting you.

Immediately, the body in the machine has returned us to each other. In this interchange there is the memory of the beach, its feel and smell, mentions of beds and sleep. Bed, a word we would never say in actual presence, a kind of touch by word we can only do with our machines. We're programmers. We send mail. It's no use trying to be other than we are. Maybe the facts of our "real" lives — his ex-girlfriend, my ex-girlfriend, all the years before we met in the group alias — mean we won't touch on deserted shorelines or across dinner tables. If so, our public selves will go on talking programs and file permissions in a separate and parallel track. If so, we're lucky for the email. It gives us a channel to each other, at least, an odd intimacy, but intimacy nonetheless.

He ends with, "We should do it again soon . . ." I reply, "Would love to." *Love to.* Who knows. The world is full of storms and beaches, yes? Below, I leave the two interpolated signatures:

— K

   — E

The Associated Press reports that the Coast Guard has turned off its Morse code equipment.[5] At 7:19 p.m. on Friday, March 31, 1995, stations in Norfolk, Boston, Miami, New Orleans, San Francisco, Honolulu and Kodiak, Alaska, made their final transmissions and simultaneously signed off. "Radiomen" would henceforth be called "telecommunications technicians." The dots and dashes of S-O-S would no longer be the universal message of disaster. Ships at sea would now hear about storms and relay distress signals via the Global Maritime Distress and Safety System, which includes "a satellite-relayed signal giving the ship's location" — many signal repeaters lining America's beachfronts, no doubt.

Veteran radiomen gathered to mourn the passing of the Morse code. "Dots and dashes are probably the easiest things to detect bouncing off the atmosphere," said one; and I remembered how, on stormy nights, Eugene would resort to code, which he liked to say aloud as he transmitted, pronouncing it "dit-dit-dot, dit-dot." One ten-year radioman, Petty Officer Tony Turner, talked about losing the feel of the sender. The transmission comes "through the air, into another man's ear," he said. The code has a personality to it, a signature in the touch and rhythm on the key. For Turner, the signature's origin is no mystery. "It's coming from a person's *hand*," he said.

ENDNOTES

1. FTP stands for "file transfer protocol," a standard method for transmitting computer files between machines on the Internet. The "IP address" is the Internet Protocol address, the unique identifier of an Internet-connected computer, or "node." After transferring a file from an FTP site, the recipient usually creates local files and directories using a program called "tar," which creates archives. (The program name is derived from "tape archive"; tapes are rarely used these days, but the device lives on in the command name.) "Tar files" are therefore named after the program that processes them.

2. The names of email commands themselves demonstrate why and how UNIX has become "arcane." A logical, clear name for an email command would be something like "electronic_mail." However, UNIX is designed for programmers, people who type, and the goal is to create program names and commands that can be invoked with the fewest number of keystrokes. Therefore, "electronic mail" became "elm." The problem is that the shortened name acquires a new association: trees. So, when a later email program came along, it was called not "mail" or "email" but, inevitably, "pine." Longtime users don't find it at all strange to use a program named "pine:' But novices certainly think it's odd to start sending mail with the name of a tree.

3. There are many "visual programming" tools now available which enable users to create programs with a minimum of coding in computer languages. In place of code, programs are assembled mainly by clicking on icons and dragging things around on the screen. However, these visually oriented tools are not in the workbench of software engineering; engineers may create such tools but generally do not use them. Increasingly, the engineering language of choice is C++, which even longtime engineers find syntactically "ugly." Below is a C++ code sample. It is excerpted from a programmer joke called "The Evolution of a Programmer," which has been circulating on the Internet. Although part of the joke is to make the code as complex as possible (it is possible to write these instructions more simply and clearly), the sample does demonstrate how far from point-and-click lies the language of software engineering.

```
#include <iostream.h>
#include <string.h>

class string
{
private:
    int size;
    char *ptr;
public:
    string() : size(0), ptr(new char('\0')) {}
```

```
    string(const string &s) : size(s.size)
    {
       ptr = new char[size + 1];
       strcpy(ptr, s.ptr);
    }
    -string()
    {
       delete [] ptr;
    }
    friend ostream &operator<<(ostream &, const string &);
    string &operator=(const char *);
};

ostream &operator<<(ostream &stream, const string &s)
{
    return(stream << s.ptr);
}

string &string::operator=(const char *chrs)
{
    if (this != &chrs)
    {
       delete [] ptr;
       size=strlen(chrs);
       ptr=new char[size + 1];
       strcpy(ptr, chrs);
    }
    return(*this);
}

int main()
{
    string str;

    str = "HELLO WORLD";
    cout<<str<<endl;

    return (0);
}
```

The code above prints the words "HELLO WORLD" on the screen in plain text. The very same functionality can be accomplished using BASIC (a programming language no longer used by "real" engineers) in a program containing the following two lines:

```
10 PRINT "HELLO WORLD"
20 END
```

4. The current paradigm in software engineering is "object-oriented programming." In this model, programs are designed and written in units (encapsulated segments of instructions and data) that can be related and reused in complex ways. Objects are combined to create components at various levels of granularity, from a small object that checks a single character to one that runs an entire spreadsheet routine. Although there is much obfuscation in discussions about object orientation, it can logically be understood as an attempt to treat software as if it were hardware — as assemblies of standard parts.

5. Joe Taylor, "End of Morse," 31 March 1995, The Associated Press. Dateline Norfolk, Va. Emphasis added.

SARA STANTON

Sticks and Stones

From ENGS 104, Fall 2010

To me, as an aspiring writer, words are a form of geography. I explore them, trace their origins, and connect them between roads of letters. Of course, there is territory undiscovered, mysteries and complex linguistic puzzles I've yet to understand. Part of my attraction to language is the knowledge that there will always be more words I don't know than words I do know. And then, much more threatening, there are words that tear at the fabric of language and culture. Words are not stagnant. Meaning is ever-changing and a natural part of language. However, this change can be dangerous as certain words evolve into derogatory slurs. I am particularly sensitive to pejorative language because it often applies to me and has affected me in immense ways.

In high school I struggled with the idea of being gay. This struggle was not confusion in knowing whether or not I was gay; it was a concrete fear of opening up about my sexuality. I had always known, and while it was a relatively quiet issue throughout my education, it was an everyday issue in social circles. "Dude, stop being a faggot," I could hear my friend James say at dinner. I would laugh with the group, careful not to draw attention to myself. While that was just another conversation to those kids, it was beyond uncomfortable for me. I played that conversation, and the hundreds of others like it, over and over again in my head. To James it was nothing, but to me it reinforced the notion that there was something wrong with me, something I could never tell a soul without becoming a social pariah. My internal homophobia eventually overcame my fear of external homophobia, and I now rarely think of my sexuality as anything other than a trait, a small piece of who I am. However, the derogatory words I so often heard in high school are still commonplace at UVM. As open and accepting as we are as a community, the use of derogatory language is startling. Just yesterday, my friend said, "That's so gay," when he found out more cops were hired in Burlington to regulate noise complaints. Now, I've grown accustomed to keeping my mouth shut in situations like this, because I don't want people to always associate me with being gay. But it was one of those days, so I responded, "What's gay about that?"

"Oh, no, not gay like you," he began, "gay like it sucks."

"Right," I replied. "So being gay sucks?"

"No no no," he explained, "it has nothing to do with being gay. If I say something is gay it's not because I'm homophobic. Obviously I'm not homophobic; you're one of my best friends. It doesn't mean that, it just means it sucks."

I couldn't help but laugh at how ridiculous it sounded.

"All right, jackass." I chuckled.

"Why am I a jackass?" he asked incredulously.

"Oh, not jackass like you're being a jerk, it doesn't mean that. It means friend now."

"Oh, I get it." He smiled.

I believe that many people aren't trying to be homophobic when they say something is gay or someone is a faggot, but that's not an excuse. We are all responsible for our actions and our words. Ignorance does not mean you are exempt from responsibility. If you don't know what a word means, don't use it. A lot of people don't know that the use of the word faggot associated with gay men is extreme, intense, and rooted in pure hate. Sure, if you ask someone what faggot means they would probably know that it originates in referencing a bundle of sticks. If you ask someone to elaborate on why a bundle of sticks was used to reference gay men, there is a gray area. In fact, the bundle of sticks is believed to refer to the burning at the stake of homosexuals. In fact, in Europe, when witches were being burned at the stake, gay people were literally used as kindling to keep the fire going for the witches.

This is only one example of words transitioning in meaning, and homophobia is not the limiting factor. Almost every group is targeted by the misuse of language. I intend to focus on homophobia simply because I am closest to it on a personal level. In exploring examples of homophobia, the most common phrases seem to be, "That's so gay," "No homo," and any incorporation of the word "faggot." On the first level, "That's so gay" is usually used to describe a situation, not a person. Then, "No homo" is used to defend the speaker, clarifying that a previous statement does not make him or her gay. Finally, "faggot" is usually used on another individual. This means that between three common phrases, almost anything that exists can be correlated to homosexuality in a negative way. Six words can degrade an entire population of people. My argument is that individuals need to be responsible for their language. If people were more sensitive about these words, I strongly believe the individual struggle with homophobia would be reduced greatly, creating a more accepting, diverse environment.

This behavior is easily perpetuated, and more difficult to stop. For example, this summer I was working at a highly regarded marine biology environmental research laboratory. One of the principle investigators was sitting with me at a family dinner in the dining hall, and as I described a story to him about a failed experiment, he replied, "Well, that's sort of gay." With his twelve-year-old son sitting next to him. Children constantly take cues from their parents, and while it may seem minute to his father, this boy now has confirmation that it is okay to use this kind of language.

While hearing homophobic slurs is common, hearing someone stand up to these slurs is rare. In fact, the only and most annoying time I ever hear anyone recognize that what they've said is wrong, is when they remember that *I'm* gay. Just yesterday I was sitting outside the library and my friend looked at a kid and whispered, "That kid is such a faggot." I didn't react, but he immediately grabbed my shoulder: "No offense, I didn't mean like that," he clarified. It is far more offensive when someone recognizes their comment as offensive only because I'm gay than simply being too naïve to comprehend the connection. When I asked him why he called the kid a faggot, my friend said it had nothing to do with being gay. "So why did you apologize?" I asked. He couldn't explain it, but he promised to try to use the word less.

The more we give these words a negative connotation, the harder it will be for people to come out. I remember when I was coming out, I didn't know how to say it because the words have taken on such a negative meaning. Now that the word "gay" can be synonymous with "sucks," I didn't want to use that word. Almost every example made me cringe, thinking of the various associations. It might not seem like a big deal to some people, but coming out can be a painful process and trying to find the right words is important and almost impossible. The added pressure of finding new words that don't feel abrasive was, for me, painstaking.

An interesting perspective is also *who* is allowed to use these words. In many cases, the perpetrator is actually gay, acknowledging that he or she can use the word because it applies to them. This is wrong, and proof that everyone needs to be educated and homophobia is not limited to heterosexuals.

Overall, my position is that this language makes it harder for people to come out, degrades the fabric of culture, and is absolutely offensive beyond explanation. All people should be accountable for their language.

PROJECT 2

Inquiring into Places and Events

COURTNEY MORENO
Fed to the Streets

From *L.A. Weekly*

My partner takes a long drag on his cigarette and scratches the back of his head. I stand with hands in pockets, my head cocked to one side. We are silent. We are staring. We face the object in front of us almost as if we are at an altar praying, so deep is our reverie.

The rig is new. New! Crisp, clean walls with our company's logo and colors painted on both sides, bordered by gleaming chrome and perched on tires with fresh tread. No scratches, no dents, no scrapes. Shining like an egg in the sun. The sirens and brakes haven't yet experienced Code-3 driving; the inside compartments, newly stocked, have not heard screaming, gasping, puking, crying; the gurney hasn't yet been contaminated with Code Yellow or Code Brown; and blood has not yet dripped onto the floor.

My eyes slowly scan the rig from top to bottom, soaking in every detail. I feel strangely, a little sick to my stomach. Is this sparkling new ambulance mocking us? I don't want to be reminded of what our last rig went through. I don't want to think about what this one is about to go through. I don't want to remember the particularly bloody trauma call two months ago, and how my partner had complained for weeks because blood had seeped between the metal floor plates that lock the gurney in place. I don't want to think of the smells I occasionally noticed in the back — old, lingering smells. We survived all that, the rig, my partner and I. We got through it together. Now, here's this ridiculous rookie rig, all clean and eager and unaware.

The station phone rings, the loudspeaker blaring right behind us. In the old days I would have jumped, panicked, bolted for the passenger seat, grabbed the radio and my map book, stared at my pager for the address and type of call. But these are not the old days, so says the fresh ambulance in front of us. I toss the keys to my partner, who drops his cigarette, crushes it. I let out a long sigh. Then we slowly walk to the doors and get in.

First call of the day. It begins.

FUMBLE

You are young, eager, a rookie, and you don't yet know that this job does not mean saving lives. You haven't yet figured out that ninety percent of all 911 calls are BS, so every time you hear dispatch say your rig number over the radio, your heart does a front flip into your mouth, all that extra weight just sitting on your parched tongue. You scramble with the Thomas Guide. You aren't good at mapping yet. Your partner may or may not hate you, and the firefighters all but roll their eyes at you as you fumble, fumble, fumble.

Your first call, the first real call, is a two-vehicle accident and an overturned truck whose wheels are still spinning as you arrive first on scene. Your partner checks the truck while you squat next to the crinkled, folded car. Your patient sits slightly dazed amid the chaotic mess. Your patient asks for water, asks if he can call his fiancée, asks if he can go home. But you don't answer his questions or say much, because as soon as your eyes connect with his against the backdrop of What He Just Went Through.

There's light behind him

Every bit of medical information you ever had flies out of your head. You used to know the difference between pleural effusion and pericardial tamponade, but at the moment you don't know your own name, much less how to make an assessment. Your eyes are locked with his, he seems calmer than you feel, despite the blood on his face and arms, the pieces of glass still stuck to him.

Does he know can he feel

Your brush jacket is too big and the helmet keeps slipping down over your eyes. You feel like a little kid playing dress-up, and it doesn't help that you could swear you see something that doesn't make any sense.

I swear I can see I swear I can see

Already you know you are too sensitive for this job, not tough enough, too trusting. You've been laughed at before for dutifully taking the blood pressure of a patient obviously faking an illness. But patients appreciate that you are all sympathy and that you actually listen to what they're saying. What you need to learn is how to focus on what needs to be done in the short time you have.

I can see does he know

And it's frustrating because you know you have potential, you know you could be good at this job but you just can't put the pieces together fast enough.

I can see his

Or detach yourself like you know you need to.

There's so much light

Because in this job to help someone you kind of need to ignore them, don't you.

I can see so much

The fire truck and the paramedic squad are pulling up lights and sirens and you open your mouth to tell him that he can't have water because it's an airway compromise, that he has to go to the hospital because he may have sustained serious internal injuries, that the paramedics are here to help him. But what comes out instead is, "I can see your guardian angel. You're going to be fine."

HALF-MAST

"Baby girl," he says. He is unable to keep his eyes open, but he's trying; his eyebrows are pulled up like ship sails trying to catch a breeze. "Baby girl, I'm not okay." I nod sympathetically, fighting the twitch his words induce in my stomach, and the flush in my cheeks. It's not that he's so good-looking, necessarily, but his low tone is personal and intimate, and there's something about those two words and the way he says them that is getting to me. If he had called me baby, babe, sweetheart, chick, darling, lady, queen, hot stuff, foxy — I've heard them all — I would've rolled my eyes, stiffened and put on my tough-girl act, but his soft, sad crooning is making me wish I had someone to go home to at the end of this shift.

I awkwardly pat his shoulder. "What happened, sir?"

When we pulled him out of the bushes twenty minutes earlier he was alone, had no wallet or ID, and was utterly incapable of answering any questions, this comical, towering six feet three inches, spilling over both ends of the gurney. Now at the hospital, the largest rag doll I've ever seen is coming to life.

He shudders slightly and his eyebrows relax, eyelids drifting shut.

"I lost all my money," he says sadly. "I gambled it away."

I nod even though he can't see. "What did you take?"

He tries to remember. He'd been drinking for twelve hours straight, and took seven pills given to him by friends throughout the night. One or two of the pills were Ecstasy, but other than that, he can't remember a thing. Which, it sounds like, was the point.

"Baby girl," he says again. He is fumbling for my hand now, and as he grasps it I really am blushing, amused and caught off-guard by my vulnerability. He rolls his head to look at me. It's a fluid, slippery motion only drunks are capable of, and for a minute it looks like his head will keep rolling right off the gurney. With supreme effort he keeps his eyes open, and then peers at me solemnly.

"Baby girl. I'm sorry."

GSW

The only time I've ever dreamed about a patient, I held the potent images in for as long as I could and was scared to share them. Some things are precious. The patient was a GSW: gunshot wound. The patient was found lying face-down in the street, with a river of blood coming out of his head. The patient was about twenty-five years old; the patient was a heavily tattooed John Doe; the patient was presumably a gang member.

Police were on scene long before we were, and they didn't bother to call it in because they assumed he was dead. They staged out the area, put up the caution tape, and started hunting for clues, witnesses, the killer, and the weapon.

At some point someone noticed that blood bubbles were popping out of his mouth, that he was still breathing.

For those of you who want to know, it looks exactly like the movies. I had trouble watching graphic movies before I drove an ambulance, and I can't watch them now. Funny, I guess, that most people can't do this kind of work, but can watch those movies without a problem.

We descended on him eagerly — a true case of trauma is a rare and coveted event — and the police officers watched with bemused interest. One even got a notebook ready in case the guy regained enough consciousness to reveal his or his assailant's name. It was my first GSW and I was very much a rookie at the time, but even I could've told the cop to put his notebook away.

The bullet had gone through the patient's occipital lobe, and the larger exit wound showed that it had shot out of his left temporal lobe. The part of his brain that controlled his breathing remained, amazingly, intact. Once we had treated, packaged and begun our transport to a trauma center, there was nothing to do but sit and watch him breathe. I matched his respirations with the bag-valve mask to help push extra O_2 in. His vitals were fine, but we all knew we were looking at a dying man, or a comatose one. His body had yet to admit the obvious.

When we went over a bump in the road, the trauma dressing slipped from his forehead, and a large geyser of blood and brain gushed from the exit wound. I yanked my left hand out of the way and slid my foot away from the new pool of blood. My right hand continued to bag him with oxygen as I reached for a new multitrauma dressing. *I saw brain*, I kept thinking.

I had the strangest feeling while watching him. His body was still warm and strong. His clothes had been cut off and he lay there oozing with life, impossibly alive. *Somebody loved him*, I thought. His mother, his girlfriend, his brother, his friend. Somebody thought he was invincible. He had thought he was invincible, clearly. The muscle memory in his body reeked of it.

Later, when it was over, when I had changed into a fresh uniform and finished my report, I took a nap in the ambulance, my arms crossed over my chest, my sunglasses on. I looked tougher than I felt. I was shaken to my boots. He died amid the tools, machinery and impersonal language of the ER. All that yelling across his body, but nothing anybody did seemed related to him. And where was he in the midst of it all? Forgotten. A John Doe, dead. A policeman's empty notebook page.

My partner didn't think he was worth saving. His opinion was that all gang members were a cancer on society, and they should be rounded up and allowed to kill each other, so the rest of us could be free of them. He had two years' experience on me and ordered me around constantly. That day I was too numb and exhausted to tell him what I was convinced of: that it wasn't our job to decide who lived or died. That I didn't ever want it to be my job to decide. If a person lay dying in front of me, I would try to help.

I didn't think I'd be able to fall asleep sitting in the rig, but in the end I did. I slept and I dreamed. In my dream there was a clean white room: white walls, tile floor. John Doe was lying on the floor, still naked but cleaned up: no sign of blood or brain or even the wound for that matter, and his skin and tattoos were gleaming. His eyes were closed, he wasn't yet dead but not alive either, and whatever life existed in him was in the form of a kind of coiled-up and angry tension; some part of him refused to let go.

I got underneath him very carefully. Curled up in a ball, my head lowered, my breathing labored, I inched his torso into a sitting position by leaning my body weight into his back and pushing the ground away. It was slow, meticulous work and he was unnaturally heavy. His arms were relaxed at his side and his head was tilted back resting on my serpentine spine. His mouth was ajar and through the open channel of his throat came a kind of smoke or light. Every time I nudged him, his body relaxed a little more, and that strange substance slid out, curling up into the air around him.

That smoke, that light was grateful to be going. It was grateful to be going, and the more it left him, the lighter and more relaxed his body became. No tension, no ugliness, no holding on. Just a body on a tile floor, with smoke and light in the air around it, and me crouched underneath.

I want to be that grateful when I go.

OUR PHANTOM LIMBS

We drive her home in the middle of the night, but she can't remember her zip code or any cross streets. The hospital face sheet only has a numeric address, and there are so many streets with that name in the Thomas Guide, running east, west, north, south, and diagonal — what side of the city did she live on? Then I have the bright idea to call someone who knows her. I pull over on the big vacuous street, a half-mile from the hospital, and set my hazards blinking. Once in a while a car zooms by and the rig slowly rocks from side to side. My partner in the back is digging through the patient's purse and finds a tattered piece of paper with a phone number on it; I dial it on my phone, forgetting that it's the middle of the night, not recognizing the New York area code, and wake the woman up. Her voice, brittle and paper-thin over the bad connection, grows with warmth and volume as the conversation progresses; she didn't know her sister was in the hospital. She helps me out with the address, then, with a choke in her voice, says, "Tell her to call me when she gets home. Please?"

I assure her, hang up, put the paper slip back I drive again, my hands at a perfect ten and two on the wheel. I know where I'm headed, easy does it, this is a simple transfer, I'm just tired, no problem, but before I know it, one tear rolls down, and then another. Ridiculous, I say out loud. I wipe my face and say it again, softer and under my breath. Ridiculous. I hope my partner doesn't see or hear me being a fool up front, but then I stop caring about that and give myself over to it. The tears flow steadily now; I have no idea where they're coming from or why. Something about that concerned voice on the phone, and the empty, dark streets, and the sad, lonely character in back, the one who doesn't remember where she lives, who didn't tell her sister about her medical problems, who is now a double amputee.

When we get to the house and struggle to fit her through the narrow, cluttered hallways in her new wheelchair, she tells us to lock the door on our way out; there are seven dead bolts and nothing inside worth stealing. I remind her, with a sense of responsibility and my own familial guilt: call your sister, okay? She looks at me, nods reluctantly, and, just before we squeeze ourselves out and into the night, gasping for fresh air, I see her pick up the old rotary receiver and stare at it.

WeThemUs

We eat fried chicken, potato chips, burritos, pizza. We microwave a frozen dinner and follow it with ice cream. We drink coffee, soda, energy drinks, liquid crack. If caffeine via IV were available, we would jab it into our veins; if filling meals existed cheaper than five dollars, we would consume them unapologetically. We smoke cigarettes right outside the hospital, chew tobacco and spit it into cups, careful not to stain our uniforms. We get scattered sleep but have perfected cat-napping: we know how to park the rig in the shade, lean the seat back, and even in our sleep, we can filter noises from the radio, only waking when Dispatch calls our rig number. We fry our brains on television and video games during the day at station. We sleep as hard as we can for as long as we can, knowing we will never make it through the night, knowing there will always be at least one call. We know how to stumble out to the rig with a half-buttoned shirt, peer sleepy-eyed at the map book, flip on lights and sirens, drive relentlessly fast, and get on scene within time. Get there and have the shirt tucked in, gloves on, equipment ready. Get there and be alert, helpful, polite. Stumble back to sleep when it is done. In the morning there is coffee. In the morning there are bags under our eyes. In the morning we have dry skin, wrinkled uniforms, our first cigarettes. Meanwhile, the firefighters are switching out crews and the fresh ER hospital staff are just arriving, pouring coffee, hearing stories of the night before.

Our patients have diabetes, heart problems, chronic respiratory disease, renal failure, hypertension. Often they have spent years killing themselves slowly with their vices; their lists of medicines are long, their trips to the doctor often. Their pain scares them, wakes them in the night, and their fear of dying lives under their skin like a parasite. They feel it is unfair, their poor quality of life. But they remember to bring their cigarettes to the hospital even when their ambulance ride is spent wheezing. They sit and watch TV on tiny beds, complaining of non fatty, compartmentalized food, even as their feet grow bluer from pooling, noncirculating blood. They stare blankly at the doctor when he advises them to exercise.

And we, the emergency medicine providers, the first responders, the paper pushers and gurney loaders, we hand off these patients to caffeine-ridden nurses, stressed-out and sleep-deprived doctors, overweight administrators. We hand them over and we roll our eyes and cluck our tongues: Here we go again, this frequent flyer is back, same chief complaint of chest pain. She survived this time, but we know one day she won't. One day we will be pulling her through hospital doors in a flurry of action: chest compressions, ventilations, IV bag in tow, the paramedic pushing atropine and epinephrine through the narrow tube. If it is someone we like, we will feel frustrated, sad, helpless. Come back, come back, we lost you this time, your heart finally up and quit. We told you, we tried to tell you, now there is nothing we can do.

All the same, we refuse to think of our own mortality.

Somehow it feels like the only way we can survive this job is to have these same vices as an outlet, as if the cigarettes and caffeine and cheap fast food are just as necessary as the gloves and uniform and gear. As if being able to choose what we put in our body makes our poor choices irrelevant. We think our youth will save us, but we are only throwing useful artillery to the enemy, only turning a blind eye to the shrinking distance between us and our patients.

Come back, come back!

CHIEF COMPLAINT

The patient I am treating has myriad infectious diseases and is spouting off a narcissistic soapbox tangent about what's wrong with her life, her health, my clumsy efforts to help. Meanwhile, the rig is lurching because my partner is tired and resents this patient's intrusion on his sleep cycle. It is three a.m. on a Monday night, Tuesday morning, whatever. I peer out the back of the rig at the streams of light. The police car is probably still behind us — should I have insisted that an officer ride in back with me? A moment ago, she'd been crawling up my arm, literally, demanding to see my pen and wanting to know what I'd done with her children — why had I killed them, why was I taking her to the graveyard, when she just wanted to go home.

I pictured the pen being driven into my throat, so I gulped away my sleepiness and threw my forearm into her sternum with my weight behind it to sit her back on the gurney. I looked at her with an icy strength I didn't feel and said in my best warning voice: "Hey, be nice to me and I'll be nice to you. I promise not to take you to the graveyard. Now *relax*."

My paperwork is sprawled about the rig. I'd take wrestling a psych patient over filling out paperwork any day. Name, DOB, Social Security number, medical-insurance ID, height, weight, age, medical history, allergies, meds . . . on and on. She's changed her mind three times about her home address, not to mention having given six digits for her phone number, so I give up. The most important part of the paperwork, medically speaking, has yet to be filled out. In a few minutes, I will give a report to the triage nurse, explaining who the patient is and what's wrong with her, and I still don't know what I'll say. She's violent, diseased, angry, but there is no apparent drug use. She's probably a psych patient who is noncompliant with her meds . . .

Does it hurt anywhere? I ask loudly, interrupting her rant. Where is your pain? "Fuck you. Where are my kids, you bitch . . ." and off she goes. Okay. Chief complaint: pissed off. Chief complaint: threatened an officer outside a 7-Eleven, then insisted she had severe pain that has now vanished. Chief complaint: probably doesn't have a home, so the hospital is as good a place as any. Chief complaint: bilateral full-bodied "fuck you" pain with good circulation, sensory and motor.

I'm going to die this way, I think suddenly. I'm going to catch Hep C from a patient, or tuberculosis, or, at the very least, MRSA. I will get slammed in an ambulance crash, crushed by a burning building, shot by a gangbanger, blown up by a terrorist, exposed to a hazmat leak. I make minimum wage, risk my life in a war zone, and for what?

I'm almost tearing up, I'm so self-involved. The car lights are getting blurry and the paperwork is forgotten. I look back at her to find her quietly studying me. I have treated her before, I realize with a start, when I first started doing this. I have a painful, blindingly self-aware moment: here I sit, another burnt-out EMT, with a wrinkled uniform and scuffed boots. My boots! When was the last time I polished them? Her eyes are momentarily clear and lucid and she smiles. "You're very pretty," she says.

Thanks. The rig stops and my partner ambles around the side to open the backdoor. His face is miserable as he puts on a fresh pair of gloves.

We're here, I say.

NO COMPLAINTS

Let me tell you a secret: in our job, it's better when there are things to do. The worst kind of patient is the one we can't help. Want to know the most infuriating chief complaint out there? Abdominal pain. We hate treating abdominal pain in the field. When someone has abdominal pain, whether it's mild indigestion or a life-threatening aortic aneurysm, the treatment is the same: drive to the hospital. That's it. They could have an ulcer, blood in their GI tract, kidney stones, a bladder infection, appendicitis; they could have internal bleeding from a bruised solid organ or the swollen infection of a hollow one. They could be throwing up bright-red blood or vomiting "coffee grounds" — digested blood. This could have been going on for weeks or hours. The most you can do on your way to the hospital is get an accurate description of where in the body the pain is occurring, signs and symptoms, and severity. The triage nurse takes it from there, but God forbid you finish your assessment on the rig and still have even one minute to go on your ride to the ER. That's one more minute of sitting there, listening to someone scream their head off, ask for pain medicine, tell you they're going to throw up. You can sympathize with their pain, hand them a basin, tell them no pain medicine is allowed until some tests are performed at the hospital, but what it feels like you're saying is: I'm useless, I can't help you; just sit tight in this overrated taxi and we'll get you there.

At least, that's what I thought.

I get a call for an unconscious male outside a shopping mall. That description, of a "man down," is the vaguest one out there; it can mean anything from a medical cause (syncopal episode, seizure, low- or high-blood-sugar diabetic, stroke, heart attack, drunk, or drug overdose) to a traumatic one (assault, stabbing, gunshot wound). He could be sleeping or he could be dead.

This patient is none of the above. When asked what hurts the most, where his pain is, what his reason was for calling 911, he says the same thing over and over.

"I can't function."

We walk him to the rig and sit him on the gurney inside and the paramedic and I climb in the back. The barrage of questions begins. Pain in your head, chest, abdomen? Difficulty breathing? Is there ringing in your ears, is it difficult to see, can you squeeze my fingers and wiggle your toes? Do you have heart problems or diabetes, do you feel confused, weak, dizzy? Have you fallen, been hit or bruised, can you describe how you're feeling, do you have any pain, and has this happened to you before? What have you had to eat or drink, what medications are you taking, what kind of medical problems do you have? Drugs, alcohol? Anxiety, stress, panic attacks?

"I can't function."

He's alert and oriented, knows where he is/what day it is/his name, but to every other question he says the same thing. He can't function. He's not taking meds, he ate lunch not that long ago, he feels "warm" from sitting in the sun, he doesn't want to hurt himself or anyone else, and one more thing: he can't function.

At first it's kind of funny, then it's annoying, then it's sad. The paramedic sits there, asking, asking, going through his store of medical information, the mental checklist. Interrupting, I report the guy's vitals one by one: his breathing, pulse and blood pressure are fine; his lungs are clear bilaterally. His blood is fully oxygenated and traveling to the farthest reaches of his body. His pupils are PERL (pupils equal, round, and reactive to light), his skin signs are normal, he's not altered in any way, and his blood sugar is perfect.

There is a moment of silence and we all sit there. If there were a clock, we would have heard its ticking. The paramedic is frustrated, but I am somewhat in awe. This man walked out of a shopping mall on a Thursday afternoon. He didn't make a purchase. He probably walked toward his parked car, or the bus stop, and then just stopped dead in his tracks, not knowing if he wanted to go home, stay put, or return to the mall to buy something. Not knowing if he was hungry, thirsty, tired, lonely, restless, anxious, sick, or crazy. He only knew he didn't know. It's not a medical complaint, and there isn't a thing we or the hospital can do, but all the same, he can't function. What do you do when you can't function? You call 911. Who else are you going to call?

Something criminal happens, and 911 sends the police; if there is a fire, the fire trucks arrive; he has a medical problem and here are the paramedics and EMTs; and when things are real bad, you get all of the above. But when someone's mind starts to go, there is no system in place. If you can't function in this society, you'd better have friends and family, because otherwise, you are shit out of luck.

In the end we take him to the hospital. I sit in the back and don't say a word. I keep thinking of a clock for some reason, the one that would be ticking because it is so quiet. The one we don't have.

CRACKED

Hail Jesus God our Father please save him, save my baby let him live please . . .
I glance in the rearview mirror. I have only a blocked view of what is happening in the back, but I hear all kinds of noise, not to mention the patient's wife is sitting in the passenger seat praying her head off. My hands are gripped tight to the wheel and I am still pouring sweat from struggling with the 280-pound patient. The one who went from dead to combative as we loaded him on a backboard and attempted to walk him down a steep flight of stairs to the ambulance waiting below. The one found pulseless, his last dying breath escaping out of his lungs as his eyes went limp.

Someone had bagged him with oxygen immediately and I had jumped on compressions. Locked my arms, leaned my full weight into the heels of both palms, pushed down to a depth of two inches, then released completely, counting to thirty at a rapid rhythm similar to that of the disco song "Staying Alive." Compressions are simple enough to do but horribly grotesque, too. They don't tell you in CPR classes that you will hear the sound of ribs separating from sternum, followed by strange squelching noises that emanate from the chest cavity. Luckily, that didn't happen with him. Luckily, his heart had a shockable rhythm and between two shocks, drugs pushed through an IV, and immediate CPR, he had actually come back.

All the while his wife had been yelling at him in an unbelievably commanding voice, "Breathe, big man! Breathe baby!" I had thought at the time, with complete absurd sincerity, that we should bring her to every full arrest from now on, who wouldn't do what she says?

Four percent or less. That's how often someone actually ends up living after CPR is initiated. It's rare to get pulses back, it's uncommon to regain spontaneous breathing, but for someone to go from dead to awake is nothing short of exceptional.

Now I see huge arms flailing around and hear the paramedic's voice, not as commanding, saying "Calm down, sir. Try to relax." I turn to the wife needing to confirm a suspicion I've had since we first got on scene. She starts her story of what happened, but before she really gets through it I cut to the chase: history of drug use?

Her eyes get real wide and she uses her booming voice to say, "He does crack cocaine!"

I nod my head, fighting the inappropriate urge to laugh. So the patient in the back is a crack overdose who just got loaded up with voltage and pure adrenaline. No wonder he's swinging and frothing at the mouth.

Please God let him go to rehab, he's been clean for two years God don't let him die for this mistake, please God praise Jesus let him live let him live . . .

After we got his pulse back our next step was to transport him immediately. Because he was big we had to four-point the backboard, and unfortunately the way out was so tight that we had to lift his feet up over the banister and carry him down the stairs head first, all of us squeezed together, shuffling our steps, trying to move as smoothly as possible. Halfway down the stairs, all that blood in his brain, his eyes opened and he started yelling and flailing and fighting us. He probably had no clue what happened to him. There he was, a born-again newborn, and his first view of the world after dying was a very strange angle of the night sky, our sweaty faces, and a beeping EKG monitor we had balanced on his chest.

We're finally at the hospital and I fly out of the ambulance to open the back doors. That's when I see that the walls, ceiling, floor, and doors are all splattered with a clear fluid that smells faintly of alcohol. Two paramedics, my partner, and our deer-in-headlights student riding with us today pile out like clowns from a circus car looking exhausted and overwhelmed. Someone tells me that our patient threw up four times en route to the hospital as I stand there, stunned, looking at the mess. Also, our patient managed to free himself from the backboard, and the slamming I had heard was that of the board swinging and hitting the rig walls.

"Everyone okay?"

Yes. Even on her first day in the field our student knew to get out of the way of projectile vomit.

We walk into the emergency department with our patient very much alive, sitting crazy-eyed on the gurney, a rubber airway assist still dangling out of his nose. The awaiting ER team that usually greets full arrests looks bewildered.

"Is this him?"

"Yup, it's him. He came back."

We move like a confused school of fish to get the patient into a room, unload him on to a hospital bed, disentangle wires, hang up the IV bag, hook him to the hospital's pulse ox, and so on. The lead paramedic's voice calls out over the scuffle of activity. He is looking at his run sheet for reference: "Good evening everybody, we have a twenty-eight-year-old male overdose found pulseless, v tach with agonal breathing. Epinephrine was administered . . ."

The medic continues and the last I see of our patient as the swarm closes in are his terrified eyes. He looks no closer to understanding what has happened to him.

Does he know? The biggest secret of all, has he realized it? We are selfish human beings just like everybody else. Ours is a gritty, gory, glorified service job that is up to its ears in the mucked up beauty that is human life. We do this job to help people, but we also do it for the adrenaline rush, the lifestyle, the stories, and the feeling of being needed. We do it because the human body is amazing and capable of so much, and because shifting the balance in a person's life is heady, addictive, and gratifying.

Hopefully, when he realizes we narrowly saved his life tonight, he won't mind how terribly impersonal it was.

EYES

You avoid looking at your patient, you have learned this much on the job at least: patient is ninety-five, female, complains of chest pain. The live-at-home nurse called 911 because she wasn't sure how severe the old woman's condition had become. They both speak Russian, you half-listen to the firefighters struggle with the language barrier while you hook up the twelve-lead EKG. Move the ninety-five-year-old breast out of the way, line up V4 with the mid-clavicular line, line up V6 with the midaxillary line, the rest is easy. Ma'am, we're going to take a picture of your heart, you say, knowing that she's not listening. Hold still for us, okay?

She is strong and angry; you feel it coming off her in waves. Feel it but don't see it; you still won't look at her. She is not the boss of the scene, the lead paramedic is, so you turn to him with the first copy of the EKG readout, which you wish you understood better but don't. He looks at it, nods. You start to put her on oxygen but he shakes his head. Thumbs over his shoulder. Do that on the rig, we're going to load her up and go.

Ah. Sack-of-potatoes time, you were waiting for this. She is old and weak, with light bones; there is a fairly easy path from the bed to the gurney waiting in the hall. You nod to your partner: we'll GS her, you say. You still don't know what GS stands for, but you get behind her, put your arms through her armpits, and grab her wrists. Your partner scoops up her legs: one, two, three, lift. The whole time, she is complaining loudly in Russian, and then before you can get to the gurney the ninety-five-year-old flesh-and-bones package wrapped in your arms starts writhing and her complaints grow louder. All of it too fierce for that frail frame.

Almost there, but the paramedic stops you. There has been a shift in the air, but you missed the turning point. You were busy negotiating with the carpeted stairs, the thick table legs, the vase your partner almost elbowed. The paramedic's face and voice have softened. Put her back, he says. You blink at him, feel the thin layer of sweat under your uniform, and start the shuffle back. She has slipped down and it's increasingly awkward. You hear the paramedic talking to the nurse while the firefighters pack up their gear and you strain to make out the words.

Okay. It's her choice. If she wants to die in her home, that's her choice.

Strangely elated, with respect. you place her on the bed. You know you can look at her now, so you do. She is propped up on frilly pillows, hands clasped, coal-black eyes burning fiercely into yours, white hair in a tight bun. Reserved, dignified, powerful. Go away, her eyes say. I am the boss of me.

Beautiful, you think. Thank you, you almost say, but stop yourself. You slip the image of her gorgeous face into your pocket along with the second copy of the EKG printout you'll study later, and almost skip out the door.

UNDER THE RADAR

On my partner's last day there is a heat wave, and my company sets a new record: 198 calls in less than 12 hours. Everyone is calling 911 today, everyone can't breathe, or has a splitting headache, or stood up and felt dizzy, or has chest pain. Everyone is hot and uncomfortable and anxious; the lines at the hospital in our district are flowing out the door. Firefighters are pouring sweat even with the air conditioning flooding the back of the rig, and the EMTs lining the hospital hallways look ready to pass out. Only the emergency room triage nurses remain unflappable.

"I have so much food sitting at station," I complain to him as we drive to our umpteenth call. "I don't want to have to buy lunch."

He doesn't say anything, just nods slightly in acknowledgement. But we both know I'll be lucky to get to eat at all today. By now he's familiar with my low-blood-sugar bitchiness; he'll probably help find me food at the hospital — one of those awful prewrapped sandwiches, or a little package of graham crackers — just to fend it off.

We work really well together. I've been trying to be unflappable and I'm failing at it: I'm terribly sad to see him go. Having a good partner is like breathing, blinking, or swallowing: so natural you don't even notice. Having a bad one is like an acute case of the hiccups. He and I have worked together now for about four months, and he's my third regular partner. We've only had a couple minor hiccups.

The scene of our umpteenth call is a residential street with a church on the corner, and when we get there we have trouble finding our patient. As the fire department pulls up, I'm looking at my pager patient details: forty-eight-year-old male, behavioral. I start scanning this peaceful intersection for someone who fits the description. This kind of situation always amuses me. It feels odd to be standing on a street corner next to a large lit-up vehicle, with gloves and uniforms on, looking at pedestrians with questioning eyes: *Is it you? Are you sick or injured? Do you need us?* I think healthy people probably get nervous when they see that question in our eyes.

One of the firefighters spots a regular standing arm in arm with another man, both of them silently watching us. The firefighter walks over and calls him by name, asks him if he called 911.

It takes me a while to place this frequent flyer although I know I've seen him before. Then I realize the last time I saw him, his miserable drunken face had been attached to a limp body that was crumpled at the bottom of a set of concrete stairs. He had smelled bad and looked worse, the stairwell had reeked of urine, and the worst part was, he kept apologizing. *He needs help*, I had thought as I hoisted him up and over to the gurney, mentally trying to squeeze my nostrils shut, *but not the kind I know how to give*. Getting sober momentarily wasn't going to fix his problems. But we had taken him to the hospital anyway, where everybody knew him. That kind of patient usually gets returned to the same hospital, by ambulance, within twenty-four hours of getting released.

Today he looks different. Today his eyes are clear, not bloodshot. He is standing tall, his arm firmly wrapped around the other man's elbow with an air of proud possession. His thick beard looks distinguished instead of vomit-flecked and grubby, and face is more handsome than I remember. In fact, standing sober in the hot sun, he looks beautiful.

I don't hear the conversation he has with the firefighter, but it becomes quickly clear that he has no interest in going to the hospital. They exchange goodbyes and the firefighter turns to us, saying what we already know but are happy to hear: "You're cancelled."

My partner and I put the gurney away and take our gloves off, wiping the new sweat from our faces. We climb into the ambulance and he reaches for the radio. "Wait," I say. "Not yet."

I want thirty seconds. I want a moment, this moment, to be under the radar. Dispatch thinks we're on scene still, and as soon as we tell them that we're cancelled the madness of the day will begin again.

He understands. He releases the brake and turns off the rotating red and amber lights; he puts the rig in drive, and we coast, slowly, silently. There is a feeling of suspension. We are in a bubble, a 3.5 ton bubble, gliding down the street.

Sometimes I have the reverse situation. Instead of trying to locate the sick person who blends in with a healthy-looking crowd, I see sick people everywhere. I see a kid riding a bike recklessly without a helmet, or an overweight person eating a triple cheeseburger. I see people stumbling around drunk in the middle of the day, driving like maniacs, chain-smoking cigarettes, getting into fights, and I think, *We'll be coming for you later.*

My partner turns right at the stop sign. Facing us and half a block down is the busy street loaded with speeding cars that will take us anywhere we might need to go: our station, the next call, or another district to provide coverage.

It's time.

I reach for the radio serenely; there is the feeling of suspension still. We are off the map, off the charts, in a submarine floating under the battlefield. I click the side button and in a clear calm voice tell dispatch that we have been cancelled on scene and are available. And with that, the bubble pops, my serenity becomes a lingering memory and it's like someone has pressed the fast forward button. We are off, lights and sirens. We are entered back into the system, we are fed to the streets.

ZADIE SMITH

Accidental Hero

From *Changing My Mind*

On the sixtieth anniversary of the end of World War II, the BBC asked members of the public to submit their personal war stories. These were to be placed online as a historical resource. I helped my father to write his account and then, using the material I had gathered, expanded it into a newspaper article, of which this is a revised version.

I knew my father had "stormed the beach at Normandy." I knew nobody else's father had — that job had been wisely left to their grandfathers. That's all I knew. As a child, the mildewed war came to me piecemeal through the usual sources, very rarely from him. Harvey never spoke about it as a personal reality, and the truth was I didn't think of it as a reality, but only as one of many fictional details woven into the fabric of my childhood: Jane Eyre was sent to the red room, Lucy Pevensie met Mr. Tumnus, Harvey Smith stormed the beach at Normandy. Later, in my twenties, small facts escaped, mostly concerning his year spent in Germany helping with the reconstruction. But Normandy stayed as fictional to me as Narnia. "Stormed!" — this made no sense. A sentimental man, physically gentle, pacifistic in all things and possessed of a liberal heart that does not so much bleed as hemorrhage. It is perfectly normal to phone my father around 6:30 in the evening and find him distraught, reduced to tears by watching the news.

Then one recent adult summer, I happened to find myself in Normandy, visiting an American poet. She was writing a verse sequence about the layers of social history in the area and took me on a day trip to the beach, where we swam and sat in the sun. It was stupidly late into my swim before it occurred to me that this might be the beach Harvey had landed upon, fifty-nine years earlier. I mentioned it to the poet, and she asked after details I was shamed to admit I didn't have. Our day turned historical. She showed me Juno Beach, the cliffs in which the snipers crouched, the maze of hedgerows that proved so lethal. Finally, the American cemetery. Thousands upon thousands of squat white crosses, punctuated by the Star of David, line up in rows on the manicured grass. You can't see the end of it. I'm my father's daughter: I burst into tears.

I returned home, full of journalistic zeal. I bought a Dictaphone. This seemed like half the job done already. I was the gutsy truth seeker, uncovering the poignant war story of a man who found it all too painful to talk about. Except I found my father not especially resistant to the idea. True, he had never really spoken about it — then again, I had never really asked. He laid out a fish lunch in his garden in Felixstowe and carefully set up the microphone on its little stand.

"It's funny you mention it, actually." Why was it funny? "Well, I've been thinking a bit about it, what with the anniversary. It's only now that I've started thinking: I would like my lost service medals back ... you know, for next year. Just be nice, wouldn't it." But why didn't you ask for them back, years ago? "Well ... they charge you for them, don't they," said Harvey doubtfully, and returned to filleting his grilled sole.

A struggle my father has always had: between hating war and having been in one, between being committed to, as he puts it, the future, and at the same time not wanting to be entirely forgotten. I think he was surprised, at this late hour, to find he wanted his medals back. I was surprised I wanted to see them. A kindly veteran who lives opposite helped us send off the necessary paperwork. When the medals arrived, I came up to Felixstowe and we sat about staring at them. These moon rocks laid out on the kitchen table.

I was a bad journalist to my father, short-tempered, bullying. He never said what I wanted him to. Each week we struggled as I tried to force his story into my mold — territory previously covered by *Saving Private Ryan* or *The Great Escape* — and he tried to stop me. He only wanted to explain what had happened to him. And his war, as he sees it, was an accidental thing, ambivalent, unplanned, an ordinary man's experience of extremity. It's not Private Ryan's war or Steve McQueen's war or Bert Scaife's war (of whom more later). It's Harvey Smith's war. If it embodies anything (Harvey's not much into things embodying other things), it is the fact that when wars are fought, perfectly normal people fight them. Alongside the heroes and martyrs, sergeants and generals, there are the millions of average young people who simply tumble into it, their childhood barely behind them. Harvey was one of those. A working-class lad from East Croydon at a loose end. At seventeen, he was still too young to be drafted, but when he passed the recruiting office on the high street, he went inside. They took his details and told him he'd be called up when he was seventeen and six months. "Made me feel a little bit special — and when you're a teenager, that's what you want, isn't it?" In November 1943 initial training was completed. They moved to Suffolk, where Harvey joined the 6th Assault Regiment RE and was mobilized the week after Christmas. "That meant our unit were officially at war. I think that's right. It meant that they could shoot you if you deserted, or something."

There followed six months of regimental training and tank training, how to ride in one, how to sleep under one, how to service it when it broke down. Harvey was still not expecting to see action before 1945. You had to be nineteen. When the rest of the unit moved to Calshott, he went to Felixstowe. (He ended up there once again, in the late 1990s, after his second divorce. Sometimes he refers to his life's journey as "the round-trip.")

"I was with the old buggers, like Dad's army. But I was only there three weeks. The law changed; suddenly you could be eighteen. So that was me." Harvey's war was on. He spent that last month hiding in the Fawley woods with his regiment. You can't see the stars like that in Croydon. On June 3, he listened to the final briefing with the rest of his regiment. "That's when they told us the truth, where we were going, King Beach, and when. I was hoping to be in one of the tanks. But last minute, I was assigned to be the radio man for the CO's truck. All the boys thought that was pretty funny. Me stuck alone with the CO."

On the fifth of June at about 11 P.M., they set off. They were meant to land on the morning of the fifth, but the conditions had been too dreadful. They were still dreadful — everybody was sick. In the middle of the crossing, Harvey saw his first British warship, a huge shadowed beast, moving through the water. As he watched, it shot off a broadside from its sixteen-inch guns, rocking sideways in the recoil. "I knew then. I hadn't known before. I knew this was serious."

It was not to be as serious for Harvey as it had already been for thousands. He didn't land at 6 A.M., he didn't land in a tank (many of these had grenades thrown into them and "brewed up," exploding from the inside) and he didn't land as an American at Omaha. Though he didn't know it, already he was steeped in luck. He approached the relatively quiet King Beach at midday and waited while his CO argued with an American general onboard who was convinced it was too dangerous to land. It was two hours before he drove onto the beach. So much experience that should be parceled out, tenderly, over years, came to my father that day, concertinaed into twenty-four hours. First time he'd left England. First time he'd been at sea. First time he'd seen a dead body.

"I was looking out from the back of the truck. Young dead Germans were everywhere. They looked like us; they could have *been* us. It was gruesome. And we'd heard by then that Major Elphinstone, our major, had died the minute he hit the beach. He stuck his head out of the tank to look about and — pop — a sniper shot him in the face. But you must write that I had an easy day. I had absolutely an easy day. The work had been done, you see. It'd been done. I wasn't like Bert Scaife."

Who?

"He was this bloke, he was a legend by the end of the day — caught so many men, shot all these mortars off — he got decorated later. I was no Bert Scaife. Not by a long way."

Harvey's truck rode up the lanes, unharmed. There were dugouts everywhere and people shooting at him, but with the help of the radio and excellent information, they made it safely through the worst. They stopped at a monastery that had been commandeered by the Nazis and now stood abandoned. There was a dead man in Nazi uniform lying in the hallway. My father bent down to turn him over and would have joined him in oblivion if it hadn't been for his CO stopping his hand just in time. The body was booby-trapped. Coiled within it, my future, and that of my brothers, and the future of our future children, and so on, into unthinkability.

He slept that night in a fragrant orchard. And what else? "Well, I stopped in Bayeux a bit after that. Bought a pen." At this point, my patience with my father bottomed out. He looked at me helplessly. "It's so hard to remember. . . . I only remember the obscure stuff."

So now I started playing hardball; now I picked the Dictaphone up and demanded to know about the shrapnel, for Harvey has some shrapnel in his groin, I know he does, and he knows I know. A doctor found it in a routine X-ray in 1991, forty-seven years after Harvey thought it had been removed. I was sixteen at the time, EMF had a hit with "Unbelievable" and I was wearing harem pants. If he'd come home and told me he'd been a waiter on the *Titanic* it couldn't have seemed more fantastical.

"Oh, that was different. That was just after I bought the pen."

A few days after the pen incident, then, my father was again in an orchard in the middle of the night. He decided to make tea, the way you did during the war, by filling a biscuit tin full of sand and a little petrol and setting that alight. He shouldn't have done that. The flames were spotted and a mortar bomb sent over. He doesn't know how many men died. Maybe two, maybe three. I leaned forward and turned up the volume. For hadn't I brought this little contraption here for my own purposes? Not to record my father's history, and not even to write this article, but *precisely for this revelation*, for this very moment or another like it; in the hope of catching a painful war secret, in the queer belief that such a thing would lead to some epiphanic shift in my relationship with my father. There is such a vanity in each succeeding generation — we think we can free our parents from experience, that we will be their talking cure, that we are the catharsis they need. I said, But, Dad, it was a simple mistake. We all make so many at the same age, but in a normal situation, they can't lead to anybody's dying. I put my hand on his hand. "But it was my fault." "Of course it wasn't. It was a mistake." "Yes, yes," said Harvey, humoring me, crying quietly, "if that's how you want to say it."

He woke up on a stretcher in a truck, two dead Germans either side of him, picked up from some other incident. That was the end of his war for a few weeks while he recuperated in England. When he went back, in the final months of the war, he did some remarkable things. He caught a senior Nazi, an episode I turned into idiotic comedy for a novel. He helped liberate Belsen. But it's those weeks in Normandy that are most significant to him. The mistakes he made, the things he didn't do, how lucky he was. To finish up, I asked him if he thought he was brave in Normandy.

"I wasn't brave! I wasn't asked to be brave. . . . I wasn't Bert Scaife! I wasn't *individually* brave; that's how you should say it for the paper." Is that why he never spoke about it? "Not really. . . . I s'pose when you realized you were playing your part in killing ordinary people, well, it's an awful thing to think about . . . and then, well, I spent a year in Germany after the war, you see, working for the army and making friends with ordinary Germans. I almost married a German girl, from the country, with a strong jaw. Lovely girl. And in her house there was a photo of her brother, in a Nazi uniform, about eighteen. He wasn't coming home. And my mate who came to visit her with me, he turned the photo to the wall. But I said no. These were just country people. There was so much evil in that war. And then they were just people like that, simple people."

That's the end of our interview on the tape. Afterward, he phoned me up several times to reiterate one point. He wasn't brave. I said, okay, Dad, yes, I've got that bit.

During one of these conversations, I revised my earlier question to him. If he wasn't brave, is he at least proud? "Not really. If I'd been one of the medicos on beach. Or done something like Bert Scaife did, then I'd be proud, I suppose. But I didn't."

Harvey Smith is not Bert Scaife — he wants me to make that very clear to you. When he caught that senior Nazi, his fellow soldiers wanted to kill the man. It was my father who persuaded them to settle for a lesser punishment: he set the Nazi walking in front of their tank for five miles before handing him over to the authorities. It is characteristic of Harvey that he was somewhat ashamed to tell me that story. He feels he behaved cruelly.

In sum, Harvey thinks pride a pale virtue. To his mind, an individual act either helps a little or it does not, and to be proud of it afterward helps nobody much, changes nothing. Still, I am proud of him. In the first version of this article, I wrote here: "He was a man able to retain his humanity in the most inhumane of circumstances." Later I scratched it out because *humanity* is these days a vainglorious, much debased word and *inhumanity* is a deceitful one. My generation was raised with the idea that those who pride themselves on their humanity are perfectly capable of atrocity. I think I'll put instead: he didn't lose himself in horror. Which is a special way of being brave, of being courageous, and a quality my father shares with millions of ordinary men and women who fought that miserable war.

SHAWN CHILDS
A Raccoon's Tale
From ENGS 1, Fall 2010

I try to comfort the whimpering ball of fur in my hands to no avail; nothing can calm him down tonight. I try again to get a syringe of formula in him to help him through the night, but all that I succeed in doing is spilling it down his masked face and soft brown body. This is the third night in a row I've been in my basement attempting to force-feed an uncooperative baby raccoon. The reason: my mom has been a certified wildlife rehabilitator since I was six and I've been her helper, if not primary substitute, for years now — sometimes happily, sometimes reluctantly, but always consistently.

My parents have left for two weeks, and I'm in charge of everyone at home: the dogs, horses, cats, opossums, and lastly raccoons. Three days into my parents' two-week absence, I get a call about a baby raccoon found starving on the road, and I agree to take it in, although I'm already overwhelmed with chores, soccer, and ongoing obligations. I assumed after all the years helping my mom that I could take care of this one by myself without a problem. Now three nights later I'm starting to question my abilities. I've done everything that you're supposed to do with a new baby. I've dipped him for ticks and fleas, given him a bed with a heating pad underneath, and given him small doses of formula every half hour. He's increased in strength but is still clearly uncomfortable, and I'm starting to run out of ideas as to why. I don't feel like dealing with this tonight; I've already missed dinner with my friends, and now I'm going to miss my best friend's birthday party that started an hour ago, and I haven't even fed the other animals. I feel anxious and irritated, anxious at what I still have to do and what I'm missing out on, and irritated at the lack of control that I have over this situation.

Growing up in the small town of Roxbury, CT, it wasn't always easy to be the animal lady's daughter, or, as my dad refers to her, the crazy animal lady. I did my best to keep my life at home on the down low; "No I don't have a pet raccoon in the basement, or a skunk in the barn," tended to be my disclaimers. My mom was known not only for knowing anything and everything about wild animals but was also the girl on call any time there was ever an animal crisis anywhere in town. The general consensus went like this: there's a stray dog on the road? Call Janet Childs. There's a raccoon on your porch? Call Janet. There's a bat in your kitchen? Call Janet. With this kind of upbringing, you get a certain reputation as a tree hugging animal rights activist.

When I was younger, I never really minded this reputation, or minded being an animal house; on the contrary, I loved it. My older sister was never quite as open to it as I was, and I didn't understand why, until I entered junior high and suddenly wearing the horse sweaters that my mom got me wasn't cool. Slowly I began to realize the stigma that went along with being a so-called "animal lover," and it wasn't necessarily a good thing. So I changed: I wore normal sweaters and didn't have people who weren't my close friends over my house. I even laughed when other kids joked about "the stupid squirrel they hit with a rock the other day." I played soccer and became known as an athlete more than an animal kid; I joined the dance club as opposed to the animal shelter club.

I sit with the baby and stroke him as he nestles into my arm for comfort. This is day four, and he's becoming weaker. I wish he were healthier so I could put him with another litter, but I can't put them at risk. I feel bad leaving him because he cries, but I have a life and other animals to feed. I put him in his crate and wrap him in a blanket in hopes that the confines will comfort him but as I leave I hear his cries of protest. I compromise by putting him in the pocket of my sweatshirt as I feed the other babies in the basement, where he soon falls asleep. I can feel the warmth pressed against my stomach and I assume that to him it feels like his mom, like home. I don't know what to do; I need to leave, but every time I move he whimpers in protest. All I can think about is all the other things I need to do; I'm not used to sitting still for so long a period of time, and it's driving me crazy. I can already feel myself slowly losing control over everything, a feeling I can only equate with the feeling of trying to hold onto something and at the same time feeling it slowly but steadily slide from your white, strained knuckles.

One day in middle school when I had finished a riding lesson (at that time in my life I took one or two riding lessons a week) and was cooling down my horse, I excitedly chattered to my riding instructor, in an overly excited and half-minded way that only middle school girls can master, about the soccer team that I had made. After a few minutes of her listening to my banter about how *awesome* the team is and about how *awesome* the girls are, she made an off-handed comment about it being time for me to choose which lifestyle I intended to pursue. I didn't understand what she meant, so she went on to explain that once I started to do sports seriously, riding would no longer be a priority and would eventually become less and less a part of my life. I remember getting very angry with her for saying that, and now in retrospect the anger probably came from a place inside of me that knew what she was saying to be the truth, something I knew was going to happen and wasn't ready to accept. In true middle-school-girl form, I threw a fit and swore that I could do both. I swore I would prove it to her and to myself.

So life went on, and I continued riding once a week for the rest of the year. Then the next year came and I did school soccer, premier soccer, and a fall basketball team. I stopped riding lessons that fall, but only for that one fall (I told myself). The next spring I had premier soccer, track, was class treasurer and did tutoring; I cut out my riding lessons again. Middle school ended, and everything seemed to be going in super speed. In conclusion, I never did get around to starting lessons again. So much of who I was growing up was directly intertwined with the life I lived at home. Any time my mom would suggest I get out and ride or spend some time with the animals, the initial reaction I felt was irritation. This irritation, which came across as irritation at my mom, was really the guilt I felt for losing contact with that part of who I used to be. It's a hard thing to accept that you can't do it all, and that you can't be everything you want to be. The day you learn that the long-lived and long-used cliché that "you can be whatever you want to be" is not necessarily true is a sad day.

It's been five days and four nights, and I'm on my way down to the basement to check on my baby and see how he did last night. I left him at midnight the night before and haven't gone to check on him till this afternoon. I walk down the old stairs and duck as usual as the ceiling beam dips down to forehead level. I hear the typical chattering from behind the closed door from the other babies, but not the particular high shriek of mine. That's fine, I tell myself; maybe he just doesn't realize I'm here yet. I flick on the light and enter the room to a dozen hands through metal bars grasping at me, and I see that the last crate on the right doesn't have any movement at all within it. My breath catches as I start to realize the inevitable, but I refuse to go and check for fear that it might be true. I make food as I always do making an effort not to let my eyes drift and finally go to the cage. He's lying on his side, his eyes half open facing towards the door that I had just entered from. I watch in silence hoping for a breath or a movement and see nothing. Eventually I reach in and feel his stiff body, at the same time that a tear rolls down my face. I am surprised by the tear; we've lost countless animals before, and I've always been the one to take care of the situation because my mom is much more sensitive around death than I am.

I find myself sitting, holding him in a towel, stroking his fur, and adding tears to it at the same time. I didn't know what to do. I had done my best and in the end my best wasn't enough. I had cared for something on my own and had watched as it suffered and died in front of me. I found myself wondering what I could have done differently, at least stayed with him longer so that he was comfortable in the end. I think about him crying as I walked away last night, and the thought results in a new round of tears running down my face.

I ended up burying him that day. I couldn't bring myself to throw his body in the dumpster behind the vet's office where you're supposed to leave their bodies (says the DEP). I knew that I was being overemotional, but that part of me was being confronted with the same battle I've faced, and lost to, my whole life. The fact that you can't excel at everything you do. I was faced with the guilt of leaving him the night before, the guilt I felt from not giving him my full attention, of leaving him to go to a party. The knowledge that if my mom had been here, if anyone who knew more than I did was there, that he may have lived. I hadn't made enough time for anything in my life, and now the repercussion was staring at me through glazed, dead eyes.

So much of life is about finding the balance: the balance between work and fun, between soccer and school, between groups of friends, between family and friends. I'm tired of feeling like there's not enough hours in the day, tired of feeling that no matter how hard I try I find myself lacking in every aspect that I participate in. The worst feeling in the world is when it catches up with you, when something dies because you were too busy trying to make your friends happy, feed the animals, play soccer and get to your boyfriend's by ten. The worst part of it is that I don't see it ever ending, I can't picture a time in the future when I won't be stretching myself too thin.

As for now, I walk back to the house, shovel in hand, and place it in the garage. I find myself staring at it, not moving or thinking; is this what meditating is supposed to be like? Then I hear a crash in the kitchen - the dogs broke something, probably because they haven't eaten yet. My phone vibrates and my co-captain asks if I can pick her up in half an hour for practice. I'm suddenly reminded of everything I have to accomplish before I leave the house in a half hour, and then there's dinner and I have to have that paper done by. . . .

And so it continues.

ANNE GISLESON
Your Exhausted Heart
From *Oxford American*

A convoy of tour buses rolled up from St. Bernard Parish, up through the Lower Ninth Ward, and over the St. Claude Avenue Bridge. If it didn't visit the site outright, the convoy probably passed within blocks of the levee breach at the Industrial Canal, where during the storm, a barge came to rest on Jourdan Avenue near the concrete foundations of houses whose former lives were now mapped out in abject squares and rectangles, linoleum flooring still retaining the scuff and tread of their inhabitants. The nose of a yellow school bus was crushed beneath the barge, the tatters of everyday life embedded in the puzzle-patterned mud cracked around it: chairs, tables, toys, appliances, intact jars of baby food, air conditioning units, abandoned wheelchairs and walkers. The destruction went on for mile after numbing mile, all the way down to the Gulf of Mexico.

But the convoy had now crossed the Industrial Canal, going west toward downtown, and was edging along the Bywater, a Ninth Ward neighborhood a few blocks from the Mississippi River, which had little flooding but was rocked by looting and fires and months of abandonment. Then, from their plush-seated, window-tinted vantage point, the passengers — politicians or engineers or disaster tourists — looked down at a corner bar with a few dozen people on the sidewalk and seemingly hundreds more packed into the bar's midday murk. In the cool, late-January drizzle, the people gathered in loose groups on the corner seemed unclassifiable, nattily dressed retirees to tattoo-faced gutter-punks, and many of them cheered the buses as they passed, raised their beer bottles in defiant acknowledgment. The folks on the sidewalk knew what the buses had just witnessed on their tour, were aware of the incongruity of what they were seeing now at barely past noon: a party under the spent neon trimmings of an old corner bar amid hundreds of blocks of desolation, across the street from debris piles as tall as the partygoers.

It was January 28, 2006, and the city was wrecked. The gathering was a memorial celebration. O'Neil Broyard, who owned the Saturn Bar on the corner of Clouet Street and St. Claude Avenue for forty-five years had died at the age of sixty-seven on December 22. He was a victim of a subset of post-Katrina fatalities — older residents who succumbed to the heartbreak, hardship, and fatigue of life in the new New Orleans, where even the most youthful and energetic residents were overwhelmed and working at a near breaking point. When, and if, older evacuees made it back to town, many of them found their

65

houses, neighborhoods, and friends gone. For many of them, "starting over," or even the possibility of another arduous evacuation, was more than daunting, it was the finishing blow. As one elderly gentleman said to a *Times-Picayune* reporter as he stood in his flood- and mold-ravaged living room seven months after the storm, "My future is behind me now."

O'Neil didn't evacuate before the storm, but stayed behind in the leaden August heat and fetid water with a shotgun, two toy poodles, a few cats, and the chickens he'd raised himself from hatchlings. He didn't want anyone messing with his business and the properties he'd accumulated along St. Claude. In the days following the levee breaches, bars all over the Ninth Ward were being looted. My husband, son, and I live four blocks down from the Saturn Bar toward the river. We evacuated at the last minute, but our next door neighbor, Craig, who, like O'Neil, didn't leave at first either, said he knew it was time to go when he saw a man walking down Clouet carrying armloads of liquor bottles, dropping them in the street as he walked. Craig, a fastidious forensic pathologist who spent the day tidying up his garden as soon as the hurricane had passed, not realizing what was happening at the nearby Industrial Canal and what was happening all over town, kept an errant bottle of Dark Eyes Vodka as a souvenir. Another neighbor said the worst sound during the ordeal of the aftermath was the night howling of the dehydrated drunks in the water-deprived and electricity-dead Bywater. When my husband and I returned to our blasted and beaten neighborhood in early October, one of these drunks, a bedraggled and aging transvestite, staggered up to us as we unloaded the trunk of our car, a go-cup of beer in hand. "Welcome back" After exchanging a few inquiries, he got to what he really wanted to relay. "You know, I stayed. I never went anywhere." He stumbled and slurred this badge of honor. "But welcome back." Over the next few months we'd piece together what happened during those first few days and weeks, before O'Neil was taken away at gunpoint by the National Guard, which locked down the neighborhood with its Humvees and razor wire.

Life in New Orleans in the months following the storm was heavy and complicated. Layers of bureaucracy collapsed like the floors of an imploded building, one slamming against another: government, insurance, utilities, government, insurance, utilities, and you could feel the aftershocks reverberate throughout your being. On any given day, nearly every person you encountered, a cashier, waitress, co-worker, an old high-school buddy, had suffered catastrophic loss — homes or jobs or loved ones or all three. In the evenings, my husband and I would go over what we called the "Daily Calamity Report" — fresh news of disaster, who'd lost what, or was leaving town, what places we loved that had just burned down or were not salvageable, any recent political bungling or infuriating Army Corps of Engineers revelation. Though we lived in the lucky twenty percent of the city that hadn't flooded, the "sliver by the river," or if you lived farther uptown in the more affluent area, "the isle of denial," the mingled sense of urgency and despair was taking its toll, as was watching people you love evolve into strangers under the pressure.

All of this in a landscape of shredded, damaged, or destroyed signs. Literally. Upon returning to New Orleans, one of the more disconcerting civic casualties was the lack of traffic signals and street signs, though liberating in an anarchical kind of way. Billboards, if still upright, became surrealist collages as years of advertising reemerged in shredded layers. Almost all contemporary plastic signs were either gone or had had giant wind-fists busted through them. In some cases, the under-layer of old, suspended metal signs revealed their businesses' original monikers (TINA's CAFÉ on St. Claude was once again PALACE PRIDE HAMBURGERS, the sign replete with turrets) or blown-off siding uncovered the stoic, homely elegance of hundred-year-old signs painted right on buildings, like the huge DRINK REGAL BEER command that emerged down on a Chartres Street restaurant facing the levee. Hurricane as both destroyer and cultural archeologist.

Miraculously, the Saturn Bar's iconic red and turquoise sign featuring the ringed, tilted planet with its swirling surface hung undamaged, one of the few things along St. Claude Avenue that was still intact when we returned. And beneath it we'd sometimes see O'Neil, sitting in front of the propped open double doors taking a break from the clean-up, trying to catch a breeze and let in some light (as there was still no electricity on that side of the street), his two poodles skittering around the entrance. In the great mess that was everything, it was hard to tell if he was making any progress, but it was just a relief to see him there, back from his forced exile.

Most of the times I laid eyes on O'Neil, he was behind the counter, underneath the flickering black and white television. He and a skulking cat were the only animated elements in the dense landscape of bottles, ephemera, keepsakes, fetishes, and trash that had piled up in front of the bar's clouded, beveled mirror for decades. A former boxer, O'Neil's tough countenance and heavy features were somewhat blurred from a lifetime of bar-owning. He kept his dark hair short and greased and his brown eyes were still bright and wary. He often wore guayaberas wilted from his decades long battle with the Saturn's air conditioning system, one of his many projects whose fallout accumulated in tangled piles of machinery on the pool table and in the leopard print booths. Though he had a reputation for sometimes being a little ornery, over the years he was unequivocally nice to me because I was polite, blonde, knew what I liked to drink, and never ordered anything fancy. But if you grilled him about the variety of beers or cigarettes he carried, paid with a twenty dollar bill on a slow night, or if you ordered a complicated shot ("the layers, they want the layers,") then there was a good chance he'd become surly or downright belligerent.

But he didn't speak much, at least to me. The bar seemed to do the talking for him, both effusive and mysterious in its volume and range of material, open to all species of interpretation. For a long time the Saturn was known for its eccentric décor (mummy suspended from the ceiling, neon trimmed stuffed sea turtle, decades of Ninth Ward garage-sale finds) and for the wild, apocalyptic paintings of O'Neil's friend Mike Frolich. But as O'Neil's health suffered, even before the storm, the slag heaps and general mayhem of the place drove some patrons away and attracted others. Some, who only knew the place in its later incarnation, swore by the "authenticity" of its decrepit state. But to me that was akin to being intrigued by a barely comprehensible derelict at the end of a bar but never acknowledging whatever detour brought him to that place, what vibrant life he may have lived before, or what fragment of that life was still active in some bright corner of his mind, shining an indirect light on the dimness and chaos.

Before his death, O'Neil willed the Saturn to his nephew on his brother's side, Eric Broyard, who along with most of his extended family had lost everything down in St. Bernard Parish. At first, Eric just wanted to sell his uncle's crazy Ninth Ward bar. Back in the '70s, he and his family had fled that part of town for the burgeoning Parish, where folks were setting up to escape New Orleans' various and growing urban ills. After all, Eric had some good offers and he was trying to get his flooring business back off the ground and take advantage of the building boom that was about to occur. But as they began the clean-up in the requisite hazmat suits and respirators, the Broyard family unearthed signs that maybe the Saturn was more than just an old dive, a big mess they'd been bequeathed. Hidden throughout the bar were old letters requesting bar paraphernalia, testimonials from all over the world about the Saturn's significance to the letter-writer. At the moment, though, what they had was a bar filled with debris comparable to the ratio of the debris that filled the city, the whole parish.

When I first met Eric Broyard in January, he had the increasing familiar look of a lot of people around town, the tired, uneasy attitude of a man who was faced with so much inconceivable loss, that if he stopped moving, stopped working, he might just fall apart. When you passed by the bar, he was usually shoveling out the soggy wreckage or laying down vinyl floor tiles, and if he paused to speak to you his large body would retain a tense, restless posture. As Eric and his wife, son, daughter, nieces, nephews, and sisters began cleaning out the place in earnest, the neutral ground across the street from the bar filled up with refuse that they carted over in abandoned shopping carts and wheelbarrows. The Army Corps of Engineers, charged with debris removal, would clear the wide, once-grassy neutral ground away and within hours, more would emerge. This cycle was still happening nine months after the storm, stores disgorging themselves of their rotted contents and ruined fixtures onto the neutral ground along St. Claude Avenue. When people saw that Broyard was fixing up the bar, hauling out load after load of junk, people told him to stop, warned that he would ruin the character of the place, the primary draw of the bar. People started sifting through the piles, like the French gleaners, hoping for some treasure or memento. This mess was too huge and it seemed a physical impossibility that a two-room bar with an upstairs gallery could hold that much stuff. But among the picked-over slag piles, my sister found a set of twenty-odd high ball glasses and a case of Saints football-helmet car-antenna ornaments. I myself scored a cut glass fruit bowl, a promotional Sambuca ashtray, and a silk screen of an old AJ's Produce advertisement from the '60s, whose warehouse at the end of our street exploded and ignited a six-block-long wharf-fire that raged for days in the aftermath of the hurricane.

O'Neil's memorial was just a few weeks into the Carnival season, which begins every year on January 6, the Feast of Epiphany, and on the pool table, along with fried chicken and finger sandwiches were enormous king cakes from Randazzo's Camellia City Bakery. My sister Susan picked the piece of cake with the tiny plastic baby buried in it, which, of course, represents the discovery of the baby Jesus by the Three Wise Men, and promptly handed it over to me, who was six months pregnant at the time. A few months earlier, when we were all still in exile, she's the sister who had told me over a tenuous cell phone connection, "You know, I can totally believe that three-quarters of the city has been all but destroyed, but I still can't believe you're pregnant." I was thirty-seven and had taken my time with the family-making enterprise, marrying the year before, inheriting a seven-year-old stepson, and then getting pregnant during the Mexican honeymoon we returned from a few weeks before having to evacuate. Though I couldn't take part in the triumphant midday send-off for O'Neil as fully as I would have liked, with at least a few beers thrown back in the smoky clamor of the barroom, at least I had the symbolic contribution of my crowd-parting belly.

And the memorial did feel triumphant. Also raising their Budweisers to that passing convoy of buses were guys who used to box in the back room at the Saturn in the '60s, when it housed a ring O'Neil made himself, the upstairs gallery rigged to hold twenty or thirty spectators. These tight, compact men, Jimmy, Tony, and Charles, neighborhood toughs back in the day, had fled the Ninth Ward with their families thirty years before when crime and desegregation pushed too hard against their communities — mostly Italian, Spanish, Irish, and German. Crescents of tank tops visible beneath their ironed shirts, gold crucifixes around their necks, and, in one case, dangling from an ear, with cinched alligator belts and a subdued swagger, they were once again hanging out on the same corner they did as teenagers, beneath the same SATURN BAR sign, looking expectantly up and down a decimated St. Claude Avenue. One gentleman had a Tony Montana cell phone case hitched to his belt, a recent symbol of the thug life that developed from the culture that had driven these guys out to the suburbs of St. Bernard Parish in the '70s.

The gathering was palimpsest of the bar's history, revealing itself with every person I'd bump into, all of its decades represented. Among the hundreds, there was Kenny, the *Times-Picayune* illustrator who'd left his five-foot-tall Dixie beer can costume there one Mardi Gras in the early '80s because it became too cumbersome, and consequently was assumed into the bar's décor. And Jeff Treffinger, owner of the Truck Farm Recording Studios across the street, who twenty years ago was the delivery guy at the Uptown po-boy shop where I worked in high school. I had a big crush on him then, and now his high-school-aged daughter attends the school where I teach. That's the kind of thing that happens when you un-Americanly stay put where you grew up. Life starts to fold back on you. And there were clownish gutterpunks with tattoos and shredded clothes self-consciously pinned back together, who thought they'd found their level in the disturbing decay of the bar, though in reality O'Neil disliked their lack of manners and proclivity to sneak booze into the bar and hang out for hours on the purchase of a couple of Cokes. And aging hipsters, more Broyard family members and friends, more recording studio owners, artists, neighbors, all gathered for the shared purpose of honoring O'Neil and his unwitting life work: the Saturn Bar.

Though the bar's walls are crowded with snapshots of parties, parties, parties, including many for the wrap of a Nicolas Cage movie from the mid-'90s (celebrities like Sean Penn, John Goodman, and Tommy Lee Jones were also drawn to its wacked glamour and obscurity) and once you could spend evenings in the storied booths watching people come through the swinging doors and step into the transformative air of the Saturn, the place had never, ever seemed so alive. Though there were no movie stars, this gathering felt like a cinematic finale. filled with reunions and pronouncements and atmospheric import. No Uptown frat boys ordering shots of Jägermeister only to throw the glass against the wall, no tourists who'd read about it in *Esquire* or in an online travel magazine. It was the people who'd known and loved O'Neil and his bar and who, for whatever reason, were still in New Orleans five months after the storm when hundreds of thousands couldn't, or wouldn't, come back.

Above all, there was the Broyard family. They had invited everyone they knew and had done some modest advertising, but had had no idea what to expect. They were earnestly shocked by the large turnout and Eric later said it gave them the confidence to make a go out of reopening the place, even with O'Neil being gone, even with the local economy in shreds. They rushed around in black SATURN BAR T-shirts, bussing tables, taking pictures, and serving drinks, ebullient and proud, embodying the vanishing New Orleans tradition of the generational family business. O'Neil himself was even there, back behind his bar. His ashes had been interred in a brass urn and placed by the cash register, where he is forever remembered by thousands and forever at one with his clutter.

The event was a small but concentrated triumph for the city's past and maybe its future, so on that Saturday afternoon when the buses passed us by, loaded with these outsiders, come to check out our devastation, our progress and lack of it, our piles of debris and our pain, mile after mile of this complicated, colossal failure, we found ourselves speculating about the passengers' speculation. Did they think we should be out gutting and rebuilding and cleaning, not drinking, in the middle of the afternoon in what appeared to be the only functioning business for miles? But of course, it wasn't really functioning. It was merely open. Liquor licenses had lapsed after the storm and the Broyards were giving the beer away, as O'Neil would've wanted it. No commerce, just generosity and gratitude. And we weren't just partying; it was a respite from the overwhelming work of reconstruction. During those few months, immediately following the storm, when there was much concern about the city's diminished population, any critical mass of people felt strangely victorious, a desperate grab at a handful of social fabric. This memorial was a loaded moment of many loaded moments in the new New Orleans, a place and time when everything you did carried meaning, getting a piece of mail, buying a cup of coffee, walking your kid to school. The stakes were high, and everyone seemed to be making big decisions all the time. So this was what it was to live inside of history. Your exhausted heart was always on the verge of something, breaking in despair or bursting with gratitude, and your soul stretched in ways that weren't pleasant but that made you feel very alive.

The convoy of buses would continue along St. Claude Avenue, passing collapsed furniture stores, and burned-out businesses, stolen (then abandoned) city buses, and rescue boats grounded when the water finally receded. They would roll back to their hotels downtown, the ones that were open and not filled with relief workers and journalists and FEMA recipients. But first they would pass the storefronts along Canal Street from Claiborne Avenue to the river, some still closed and blank with plywood, others broken open and glittering with shattered shop windows.

MEREDITH HALL

Threshold

From *Without a Map*

An American flag, brilliant red and white and blue against the clear Maine sky, snaps in the crisp September wind. Lions lying on either side of the wide stone steps watch me pass. They know I don't belong here. I am running late for my first class at Bowdoin College. I am a freshman. I am forty years old.

A flag never holds any inspiration for me, but today it fills me with a sense of great purpose, of capacity, of change. The campus is almost empty, the students already in their classrooms. I have been up since five, have fed and watered the sheep and chickens, turning them out for the day. I packed a large lunch for Alex and Ben. I made a hot breakfast, and while we ate at the comfortable old table, we went over the plan for the day: I will be home to meet Ben's bus at three. We will grab a snack and go back to the school for Alex's four-thirty soccer game. Alex has a bag of food for before the game — another sandwich, fruit, trail mix — and his soccer bag. I tell him to run down to the drying rack for his clean shin guards. Ben has his sign-up sheet for sponsors for the free-throw contest on Saturday.

I have no degree and can't support my family. I have been working for a sheetrock company, sanding walls and making dump runs. Sometimes they get the painting contract and I roll out white paint in three coats over the raw sheetrock, a break from the sanding and dust. When there isn't enough work to keep me on the crew, I clean houses for people who leave their dirty underwear on the floor for me and don't wipe last night's grease from the stovetop. I haven't always done such demeaning work. Before the children were both in school, I stayed at home with them on our little homestead. We raised the sheep and chickens and gardens, and wandered the woods and shore and pasture. We read books and made clay towns and stacked firewood. Once the kids were in school, my husband and I rebuilt old houses for resale. But now I am on my own, and I'm scared.

At first, with no degree, I stupidly applied for teaching jobs. Then teaching assistant jobs. Then library helper jobs. Then school secretary jobs. Then lunch lady jobs. There is nothing in our small Maine town between working in the school and working as a laborer. I sand sheetrock and scrub bathrooms for a living. Today, the flag whipping in the wind, so clean and unequivocal, announces that something big has begun. I am a college student. I will graduate and get that job as a high school teacher, and I will be able to support my children. I am stirred by the snapping flag, as if it is an announcement of my new start.

I'm not just a college student. I am the only nontraditional student at Bowdoin College. I wrote a desperate letter asking to be admitted. It wasn't the first letter I had sent to Bowdoin. When Alex and Benjamin first started school, I sent a letter inquiring about going back to college. I received a cool and formal letter back, informing me that Bowdoin is not a community college, and suggesting that I attend the state university's small local campus. But I am desperate this time, and send a passionate letter: *I am turning forty this year,* I say. *All these years of Cambridge and a fishing boat and the Middle East, of a homestead and children. Of learning what it is I need to know.* I do not mention my dark and secret past, the long, strange path that has brought me here finally. *I am hungry,* I say. *I am asking for a chance to learn.* This time, a letter comes from the admissions office. *We have received your (very moving) letter of application. I am delighted to write on behalf of the Admissions Committee that you have been admitted as a student at Bowdoin.* I'm in.

Today, I hurry under the giant trees and cross the near-empty campus, feeling already the complications of also being a mother and the family wage earner. I push to the back of my mind the looming truths: Bowdoin has given me full tuition support. But I will have to cut way back on my work, and we have four years ahead of very precarious finances. In the end, I will remortgage my house to the maximum, and we will slowly eat our way to the bottom of a very deep well of debt. I will live scared for many more years. But I do not know yet just how frightening this is going to be. Today, all I know is that I have leaped onto my next new path.

My first class starts in four minutes. I find Massachusetts Hall, a small and classic brick building from the earliest years of the college. Up a delicate, curving stairwell that has somehow survived nearly two hundred years of student traffic. I hear young voices at the top of the stairs. As I near the doorway, I forget my fears about supporting my children, forget that I am here in order to gain the credentials to make a living. Suddenly, I am a student. I am a college student. I am here to finally become educated. I am starved. Suddenly, I want to cry. I am on a threshold. I understand that my life is about to change, that there will be a past, a time before I came to this place, and an after, a time in which I will make my way knowing how to feed the wild hungers that have haunted my life.

The young students look up as I enter the classroom — a white-plastered garret filled with odd chairs, the leaded windows opened to the fall day. This is a very smart place. I can feel that I am among smart people, an energy that pervades the room. The boys wear baseball caps, some backward. Their faces are open, expectant. I can see in them my own sons not long from now. The girls lounge in their chairs, confident and lively. I don't remember ever feeling like these young people, so at ease in the world. They all stop speaking for a moment, staring at me, an old woman in their classroom, the only one they will see here for the next four years. I am embarrassed, and my feelings of great anticipation deflate instantly. I forgot: I am forty years old, a girl who somehow became a woman and missed this crucial step, a catch-up woman among kids. In that hushed pause at the door, my history of shame and mistakes and decisions that threw me outside the world rushes up in me.

Then a girl smiles, the young students graciously turn back to their conversations, and I find my way to a chair in the old room. I pull out a new notebook and pencil, feeling like a child. Professor Diehl strolls confidently into the room and organizes her papers on the table. She is younger than I. "Welcome back," she says to the group with a smile. Her eyes catch mine and she doesn't hesitate. Has she been warned that I will be in her class? "The Politics of Genre. I'd like to go over the syllabus." I have never heard of a syllabus. I pay absolute attention to every word. I will graduate summa cum laude in four years, buried in debt, filled with hope and urgency, a grown woman ready to move into an unimagined new life.

PROJECT 3

Re-Visioning Choices

TIM O'BRIEN
How to Tell a True War Story
From *The Things They Carried*

This is true.

I had a buddy in Vietnam. His name was Bob Kiley, but everybody called him Rat.

A friend of his gets killed, so about a week later Rat sits down and writes a letter to the guy's sister. Rat tells her what a great brother she had, how together the guy was, a number one pal and comrade. A real soldier's soldier, Rat says. Then he tells a few stories to make the point, how her brother would always volunteer for stuff nobody else would volunteer for in a million years, dangerous stuff, like doing recon or going out on these really badass night patrols. Stainless steel balls, Rat tells her. The guy was a little crazy, for sure, but crazy in a good way, a real daredevil, because he liked the challenge of it, he liked testing himself, just man against gook. A great, great guy, Rat says.

Anyway, it's a terrific letter, very personal and touching. Rat almost bawls writing it. He gets all teary telling about the good times they had together, how her brother made the war seem almost fun, always raising hell and lighting up villes and bringing smoke to bear every which way. A great sense of humor, too. Like the time at this river when he went fishing with a whole damn crate of hand grenades. Probably the funniest thing in world history, Rat says, all that gore, about twenty zillion dead gook fish. Her brother, he had the right attitude. He knew how to have a good time. On Halloween, this real hot spooky night, the dude paints up his body all different colors and puts on this weird mask and goes out on ambush almost stark naked, just boots and balls and an M-16. A tremendous human being, Rat says. Pretty nutso sometimes, but you could trust him with your life.

And then the letter gets very sad and serious. Rat pours his heart out. He says he loved the guy. He says the guy was his best friend in the world. They were like soul mates, he says, like twins or something, they had a whole lot in common. He tells the guy's sister he'll look her up when the war's over.

So what happens?

Rat mails the letter. He waits two months. The dumb cooze never writes back.

A true war story is never moral. It does not instruct, nor encourage virtue, nor suggest models of proper human behavior, nor restrain men from doing the things they have always done. If a story seems moral, do not believe it. If at the end of a war story you feel uplifted, or if you feel that some small bit of rectitude has been salvaged from the larger waste, then you have been made the victim of a very old and terrible lie. There is no rectitude whatsoever. There is no virtue. As a first rule of thumb, therefore, you can tell a true war story by its absolute and uncompromising allegiance to obscenity and evil. Listen to Rat Kiley. *Cooze*, he says. He does not say *bitch*. He certainly does not say *woman*, or *girl*. He says *cooze*. Then he spits and stares. He's nineteen years old — it's too much for him — so he looks at you with those big gentle killer eyes and says *cooze*, because his friend is dead, and because it's so incredibly sad and true: she never wrote back.

You can tell a true war story if it embarrasses you. If you don't care for obscenity, you don't care for the truth; if you don't care for the truth, watch how you vote. Send guys to war, they come home talking dirty.

Listen to Rat: "Jesus Christ, man, I write this beautiful fucking letter, I slave over it, and what happens? The dumb cooze never writes back."

The dead guy's name was Curt Lemon. What happened was, we crossed a muddy river and marched west into the mountains, and on the third day we took a break along a trail junction in deep jungle. Right away, Lemon and Rat Kiley started goofing off. They didn't understand about the spookiness. They were kids; they just didn't know. A nature hike, they thought, not even a war, so they went off into the shade of some giant trees — quadruple canopy, no sunlight at all — and they were giggling and calling each other motherfucker and playing a silly game they'd invented. The game involved smoke grenades, which were harmless unless you did stupid things, and what they did was pull out the pin and stand a few feet apart and play catch under the shade of those huge trees. Whoever chickened out was a motherfucker. And if nobody chickened out, the grenade would make a light popping sound and they'd be covered with smoke and they'd laugh and dance around and then do it again.

It's all exactly true.

It happened nearly twenty years ago, but I still remember that trail junction and the giant trees and a soft dripping sound somewhere beyond the trees. I remember the smell of moss. Up in the canopy there were tiny white blossoms, but no sunlight at all, and I remember the shadows spreading out under the trees where Lemon and Rat Kiley were playing catch with smoke grenades. Mitchell Sanders sat flipping his yo-yo. Norman Bowker and Kiowa and Dave Jensen were dozing, or half-dozing, and all around us were those ragged green mountains.

Except for the laughter things were quiet.

At one point, I remember, Mitchell Sanders turned and looked at me, not quite nodding, then after a while he rolled up his yo-yo and moved away.

It's hard to tell what happened next.

They were just goofing. There was a noise, I suppose, which must've been the detonator, so I glanced behind me and watched Lemon step from the shade into bright sunlight. His face was suddenly brown and shining. A handsome kid, really. Sharp gray eyes, lean and narrow-waisted, and when he died it was almost beautiful, the way the sunlight came around him and lifted him up and sucked him high into a tree full of moss and vines and white blossoms.

In any war story, but especially a true one, it's difficult to separate what happened from what seemed to happen. What seems to happen becomes its own happening and has to be told that way. The angles of vision are skewed. When a booby trap explodes, you close your eyes and duck and float outside yourself. When a guy dies, like Lemon, you look away and then look back for a moment and then look away again. The pictures get jumbled; you tend to miss a lot. And then afterward, when you go to tell about it, there is always that surreal seemingness, which makes the story seem untrue, but which in fact represents the hard and exact truth as it seemed.

In many cases a true war story cannot be believed. If you believe it, be skeptical. It's a question of credibility. Often the crazy stuff is true and the normal stuff isn't because the normal stuff is necessary to make you believe the truly incredible craziness.

In other cases you can't even tell a true war story. Sometimes it's just beyond telling.

I heard this one, for example, from Mitchell Sanders. It was near dusk and we were sitting at my foxhole along a wide, muddy river north of Quang Ngai. I remember how peaceful the twilight was. A deep pinkish red spilled out on the river, which moved without sound, and in the morning we would cross the river and march west into the mountains. The occasion was right for a good story.

"God's truth," Mitchell Sanders said. "A six-man patrol goes up into the mountains on a basic listening-post operation. The idea's to spend a week up there, just lie low and listen for enemy movement. They've got a radio along, so if they hear anything suspicious — anything — they're supposed to call in artillery or gunships, whatever it takes. Otherwise they keep strict field discipline. Absolute silence. They just listen."

He glanced at me to make sure I had the scenario. He was playing with his yo-yo, making it dance with short, tight little strokes of the wrist.

His face was blank in the dusk.

"We're talking hardass LP. These six guys, they don't say boo for a solid week. They don't got tongues. *All* ears."

"Right," I said.

"Understand me?"

"Invisible."

Sanders nodded.

"Affirm," he said. "Invisible. So what happens is, these guys get themselves deep in the bush, all camouflaged up, and they lie down and wait and that's all they do, nothing else, they lie there for seven straight days and just listen. And man, I'll tell you — it's spooky. This is mountains. You don't *know* spooky till you been there. Jungle, sort of, except it's way up in the clouds and there's always this fog — like rain, except it's not raining — everything's all wet and swirly and tangled up and you can't see jack, you can't find your own pecker to piss with. Like you don't even have a body. Serious spooky. You just go with the vapors — the fog sort of takes you in. . . . And the sounds, man. The sounds carry forever. You hear shit nobody should *ever* hear."

Sanders was quiet for a second, just working the yo-yo, then he smiled at me. "So, after a couple days the guys start hearing this real soft, kind of wacked-out music. Weird echoes and stuff. Like a radio or something, but it's not a radio, it's this strange gook music that comes right out of the rocks. Faraway, sort of, but right up close, too. They try to ignore it. But it's a listening post, right? So they listen. And every night they keep hearing this crazyass gook concert. All kinds of chimes and xylophones. I mean, this is wilderness — no way, it can't be real — but there it *is*, like the mountains are tuned in to Radio Fucking Hanoi. Naturally they get nervous. One guy sticks Juicy Fruit in his ears. Another guy almost flips. Thing is, though, they can't report music. They can't get on the horn and call back to base and say, 'Hey, listen, we need some firepower, we got to blow away this weirdo gook rock band.' They can't do that. It wouldn't go down. So they lie there in the fog and keep their mouths shut. And what makes it extra bad, see, is the poor dudes can't horse around like normal. Can't joke it away. Can't even talk to each other except maybe in whispers, all hush-hush, and that just revs up the willies. All they do is listen."

Again there was some silence as Mitchell Sanders looked out on the river. The dark was coming on hard now, and off to the west I could see the mountains rising in silhouette, all the mysteries and unknowns.

"This next part," Sanders said quietly, "you won't believe."

"Probably not," I said.

"You won't. And you know why?"

"Why?"

He gave me a tired smile. "Because it happened. Because every word is absolutely dead-on true."

Sanders made a little sound in his throat, like a sigh, as if to say he didn't care if I believed it or not. But he did care. He wanted me to believe, I could tell. He seemed sad, in a way.

"These six guys, they're pretty fried out by now, and one night they start hearing voices. Like at a cocktail party. That's what it sounds like, this big swank gook cocktail party somewhere out there in the fog. Music and chitchat and stuff. It's crazy, I know, but they hear the champagne corks. They hear the actual martini glasses. Real hoity-toity, all very civilized, except this isn't civilization. This is Nam.

"Anyway, the guys try to be cool. They just lie there and groove, but after a while they start hearing — you won't believe this — they hear chamber music. They hear violins and shit. They hear this terrific mama-san soprano. Then after a while they hear gook opera and a glee club and the Haiphong

Boys Choir and a barbershop quartet and all kinds of weird chanting and Buddha-Buddha stuff. The whole time, in the background, there's still that cocktail party going on. All these different voices. Not human voices, though. Because it's the mountains. Follow me? The rock — it's *talking*. And the fog, too, and the grass and the goddamn mongooses. Everything talks. The trees talk politics, the monkeys talk religion. The whole country. Vietnam, the place talks.

"The guys can't cope. They lose it. They get on the radio and report enemy movement — a whole army, they say — and they order up the firepower. They get arty and gunships. They call in air strikes. And I'll tell you, they fuckin' crash that cocktail party. All night long, they just smoke those mountains. They make jungle juice. They blow away trees and glee clubs and whatever else there is to blow away. Scorch time. They walk napalm up and down the ridges. They bring in the Cobras and F-4s, they use Willie Peter and HE and incendiaries. It's all fire. They make those mountains burn.

"Around dawn things finally get quiet. Like you never even *heard* quiet before. One of those real thick, real misty days — just clouds and fog, they're off in this special zone — and the mountains are absolutely dead-flat silent. Like Brigadoon — pure vapor, you know? Everything's all sucked up inside the fog. Not a single sound, except they still *hear* it.

"So they pack up and start humping. They head down the mountain, back to base camp, and when they get there they don't say diddly. They don't talk. Not a word, like they're deaf and dumb. Later on this fat bird colonel comes up and asks what the hell happened out there. What'd they hear? Why all the ordnance? The man's ragged out, he gets down tight on their case. I mean, they spent six trillion dollars on firepower, and this fatass colonel wants answers, he wants to know what the fuckin' story is.

"But the guys don't say zip. They just look at him for a while, sort of funny-like, sort of amazed, and the whole war is right there in that stare. It says everything you can't ever say. It says, man, you got *wax* in your ears. It says, poor bastard, you'll never know — wrong frequency — you don't *even* want to hear this. Then they salute the fucker and walk away, because certain stories you don't ever tell."

You can tell a true war story by the way it never seems to end. Not then, not ever. Not when Mitchell Sanders stood up and moved off into the dark.

It all happened.

Even now I remember that yo-yo. In a way, I suppose, you had to be there, you had to hear it, but I could tell how desperately Sanders wanted me to believe him, his frustration at not quite getting the details right, not quite pinning down the final and definitive truth.

And I remember sitting at my foxhole that night, watching the shadows of Quang Ngai, thinking about the coming day and how we would cross the river and march west into the mountains, all the ways I might die, all the things I did not understand.

Late in the night Mitchell Sanders touched my shoulder.

"Just came to me," he whispered. "The moral, I mean. Nobody listens. Nobody hears nothing. Like that fatass colonel. The politicians, all the civilian types, what they need is to go out on LP. The vapors, man. Trees and rocks — you got to *listen* to your enemy."

And then again, in the morning, Sanders came up to me. The platoon was preparing to move out, checking weapons, going through all the little rituals that preceded a day's march. Already the lead squad had crossed the river and was filing off toward the west.

"I got a confession to make," Sanders said. "Last night, man, I had to make up a few things."

"I know that."

"The glee club. There wasn't any glee club."

"Right."

"No opera."

"Forget it, I understand."

"Yeah, but listen, it's still true. Those six guys, they heard wicked sound out there. They heard sound you just plain won't believe."

Sanders pulled on his rucksack, closed his eyes for a moment, then almost smiled at me.

I knew what was coming but I beat him to it.

"All right," I said, "what's the moral?"

"Forget it."

"No, go ahead."

For a long while he was quiet, looking away, and the silence kept stretching out until it was almost embarrassing. Then he shrugged and gave me a stare that lasted all day.

"Hear that quiet, man?" he said. "There's your moral."

In a true war story, if there's a moral at all, it's like the thread that makes the cloth. You can't tease it out. You can't extract the meaning without unraveling the deeper meaning. And in the end, really, there's nothing much to say about a true war story, except maybe "Oh."

True war stories do not generalize. They do not indulge in abstraction or analysis.

For example: War is hell. As a moral declaration the old truism seems perfectly true, and yet because it abstracts, because it generalizes, I can't believe it with my stomach. Nothing turns inside.

It comes down to gut instinct. A true war story, if truly told, makes the stomach believe.

This one does it for me. I've told it before — many times, many versions — but here's what actually happened.

We crossed the river and marched west into the mountains. On the third day, Curt Lemon stepped on a booby-trapped 105 round. He was playing catch with Rat Kiley, laughing, and then he was dead. The trees were thick; it took nearly an hour to cut an LZ for the dustoff.

Later, higher in the mountains, we came across a baby VC water buffalo. What it was doing there I don't know — no farms or paddies — but we chased it down and got a rope around it and led it along to a deserted village where we set for the night. After supper Rat Kiley went over and stroked its nose.

He opened up a can of C rations, pork and beans, but the baby buffalo wasn't interested.

Rat shrugged.

He stepped back and shot it through the right front knee. The animal did not make a sound. It went down hard, then got up again, and Rat took careful aim and shot off an ear. He shot it in the hindquarters and in the little hump at its back. He shot it twice in the flanks. It wasn't to kill; it was just to hurt. He put the rifle muzzle up against the mouth and shot the mouth away. Nobody said much. The whole platoon stood there watching, feeling all kinds of things, but there wasn't a great deal of pity for the baby water buffalo. Lemon was dead. Rat Kiley had lost his best friend in the world. Later in the week he would write a long personal letter to the guy's sister, who would not write back, but for now it was a question of pain. He shot off the tail. He shot away chunks of meat below the ribs. All around us there was the smell of smoke and filth, and deep greenery, and the evening was humid and very hot. Rat went to automatic. He shot randomly, almost casually, quick little spurts in the belly and butt. Then he reloaded, squatted down, and shot it in the left front knee. Again the animal fell hard and tried to get up, but this time it couldn't quite make it. It wobbled and went down sideways. Rat shot it in the nose. He bent forward and whispered something, as if talking to a pet, then he shot it in the throat. All the while the baby buffalo was silent, or almost silent, just a light bubbling sound where the nose had been. It lay very still. Nothing moved except the eyes, which were enormous, the pupils shiny black and dumb.

Rat Kiley was crying. He tried to say something, but then cradled his rifle and went off by himself.

The rest of us stood in a ragged circle around the baby buffalo. For a time no one spoke. We had witnessed something essential, something brand-new and profound, a piece of the world so startling there was not yet a name for it.

Somebody kicked the baby buffalo.

It was still alive, though just barely, just in the eyes.

"Amazing," Dave Jensen said. "My whole life, I never seen anything like it."

"Never?"

"Not hardly. Not once."

Kiowa and Mitchell Sanders picked up the baby buffalo. They hauled it across the open square, hoisted it up, and dumped it in the village well.

Afterward, we sat waiting for Rat to get himself together.

"Amazing," Dave Jensen kept saying.

"For sure."

"A new wrinkle. I never seen it before."

Mitchell Sanders took out his yo-yo.

"Well, that's Nam," he said. "Garden of Evil. Over here, man, every sin's real fresh and original."

How do you generalize?

War is hell, but that's not the half of it, because war is also mystery and terror and adventure and courage and discovery and holiness and pity and despair and longing and love. War is nasty; war is fun. War is thrilling; war is drudgery. War makes you a man; war makes you dead.

The truths are contradictory. It can be argued, for instance, that war is grotesque. But in truth war is also beauty. For all its horror, you can't help but gape at the awful majesty of combat. You stare out at tracer rounds unwinding through the dark like brilliant red ribbons. You crouch in ambush as a cool, impassive moon rises over the nighttime paddies. You admire the fluid symmetries of troops on the move, the harmonies of sound and shape and proportion, the great sheets of metal-fire streaming down from a gunship, the illumination rounds, the white phosphorous, the purply black glow of napalm, the rocket's red glare. It's not pretty, exactly. It's astonishing. It fills the eye. It commands you. You hate it, yes, but your eyes do not. Like a killer forest fire, like cancer under a microscope, any battle or bombing raid or artillery barrage has the aesthetic purity of absolute moral indifference — a powerful, implacable beauty — and a true war story will tell the truth about this, though the truth is ugly.

To generalize about war is like generalizing about peace. Almost everything is true. Almost nothing is true. At its core, perhaps, war is just another name for death, and yet any soldier will tell you, if he tells the truth, that proximity to death brings with it a corresponding proximity to life. After a fire fight, there is always the immense pleasure of aliveness. The trees are alive. The grass, the soil — everything. All around you things are purely living, and you among them, and the aliveness makes you tremble. You feel an intense, out-of-the-skin awareness of your living self — your truest self, the human being you want to be and then become by the force of wanting it. In the midst of evil you want to be a good man. You want decency. You want justice and courtesy and human concord, things you never knew you wanted. There is a kind of largeness to it; a kind of godliness. Though it's odd, you're never more alive than when you're almost dead. You recognize what's valuable. Freshly, as if for the first time, you love what's best in yourself and in the world, all that might be lost. At the hour of dusk you sit at your foxhole and look out on a wide river turning pinkish red, and at the mountains beyond, and although in the morning you must cross the river and go into the mountains and do terrible things and maybe die, even so, you find yourself studying the fine colors on the river, you feel wonder and awe at the setting of the sun, and you are filled with a hard, aching love for how the world could be and always should be, but now is not.

Mitchell Sanders was right. For the common soldier, at least, war has the feel — the spiritual texture — of a great ghostly fog, thick and permanent.

There is no clarity. Everything swirls. The old rules are no longer binding, the old truths no longer true. Right spills over into wrong. Order blends into chaos, love into hate, ugliness into beauty, law into anarchy, civility into savagery. The vapors suck you in. You can't tell where you are, or why you're there, and the only certainty is absolute ambiguity.

In war you lose your sense of the definite, hence your sense of truth itself, and therefore it's safe to say that in a true war story nothing much is ever very true.

Often in a true war story there is not even a point, or else the point doesn't hit you until twenty years later, in your sleep, and you wake up and shake your wife and start telling the story to her, except when you get to the end you've forgotten the point again. And then for a long time you lie there watching the story happen in your head. You listen to your wife's breathing. The war's over. You close your eyes. You smile and think, Christ, what's the *point?*

This one wakes me up.

In the mountains that day, I watched Lemon turn sideways. He laughed and said something to Rat Kiley. Then he took a peculiar half step, moving from shade into bright sunlight, and the booby-trapped 105 round blew him into a tree. The parts were just hanging there, so Norman Bowker and I were ordered to shinny up and peel him off. I remember the white bone of an arm. I remember pieces of skin and something wet and yellow that must've been the intestines. The gore was horrible, and stays with me, but what wakes me up twenty years later is Norman Bowker singing "Lemon Tree" as we threw down the parts.

You can tell a true war story by the questions you ask. Somebody tells a story, let's say, and afterward you ask, "Is it true?" and if the answer matters, you've got your answer.

For example, we've all heard this one. Four guys go down a trail. A grenade sails out. One guy jumps on it and takes the blast and saves his three buddies.

Is it true?

The answer matters.

You'd feel cheated if it never happened. Without the grounding reality, it's just a trite bit of puffery, pure Hollywood, untrue in the way all such stories are untrue. Yet even if it did happen — and maybe it did, anything's possible — even then you know it can't be true, because a true war story does not depend upon that kind of truth. Happeningness is irrelevant. A thing may happen and be a total lie; another thing may not happen and be truer than the truth. For example: four guys go down a trail. A grenade sails out. One guy jumps on it and takes the blast, but it's a killer grenade and everybody dies anyway. Before they die, though, one of the dead guys says, "The fuck you do *that* for?" and the jumper says, "Story of my life, man," and the other guy starts to smile but he's dead.

That's a true story that never happened.

Twenty years later, I can still see the sunlight on Lemon's face. I can see him turning, looking back at Rat Kiley, then he laughed and took that curious half step from shade into sunlight, his face suddenly brown and shining, and when his foot touched down, in that instant, he must've thought it was the sunlight that was killing him. It was not the sunlight. It was a rigged 105 round. But if I could ever get the story right, how the sun seemed to gather around him and pick him up and lift him into a tree, if I could somehow recreate the fatal whiteness of that light, the quick glare, the obvious cause and effect, then you would believe the last thing Lemon believed, which for him must've been the final truth.

Now and then, when I tell this story, someone will come up to me afterward and say she liked it. It's always a woman. Usually it's an older woman of kindly temperament and humane politics. She'll explain that as a rule she hates war stories, she can't understand why people want to wallow in blood and gore. But this one she liked. Sometimes, even, there are little tears. What I should do, she'll say, is put it all behind me. Find new stories to tell.

I won't say it but I'll think it.

I'll picture Rat Kiley's face, his grief, and I'll think, *You dumb cooze.*

Because she wasn't listening.

It wasn't a war story. It was a love story. It was a ghost story.

But you can't say that. All you can do is tell it one more time, patiently, adding and subtracting, making up a few things to get at the real truth. No Mitchell Sanders, you tell her. No Lemon, no Rat Kiley. And it didn't happen in the mountains, it happened in this little village on the Batangan Peninsula, and it was raining like crazy, and one night a guy named Stink Harris woke up screaming with a leech on his tongue. You can tell a true war story if you just keep on telling it.

In the end, of course, a true war story is never about war. It's about the special way that dawn spreads out on a river when you know you must cross the river and march into the mountains and do things you are afraid to do. It's about love and memory. It's about sorrow. It's about sisters who never write back and people who never listen.

BRIAN DOYLE

The Greatest Nature Essay Ever

From *Orion*

...Would begin with an image so startling and lovely and wondrous that you would stop riffling through the rest of the mail, take your jacket off, sit down at the table, adjust your spectacles, tell the dog to lie *down*, tell the kids to make their *own* sandwiches for heavenssake, that's why God gave you *hands*, and read straight through the piece, marveling that you had indeed seen or smelled or heard *exactly* that, but never quite articulated it that way, or seen or heard it articulated that way, and you think, *Man, this is why I read nature essays, to be startled and moved like that, wow.*

The next two paragraphs would smoothly and gently move you into a story, seemingly a small story, a light tale, easily accessed, something personal but not self-indulgent or self-absorbed on the writer's part, just sort of a cheerful nutty everyday story maybe starring an elk or a mink or a child, but then there would suddenly be a sharp sentence where the dagger enters your heart and the essay spins on a dime like a skater, and you are plunged into waaay deeper water, you didn't see it coming at *all*, and you actually shiver, your whole body shimmers, and much later, maybe when you are in bed with someone you love and you are trying to evade his or her icy feet, you think, *My God, stories do have roaring power, stories are the most crucial and necessary food, how come we never hardly say that out loud?*

The next three paragraphs then walk inexorably toward a line of explosive Conclusions on the horizon like inky alps. Probably the sentences get shorter, more staccato. Terser. Blunter. Shards of sentences. But there's no opinion or commentary, just one line fitting into another, each one making plain inarguable sense, a goat or even a senator could easily understand the sentences and their implications, and there's no shouting, no persuasion, no eloquent pirouetting, no pronouncements and accusations, no sermons or homilies, just calm clean clear statements one after another, fitting together like people holding hands.

Then an odd paragraph, this is a most unusual and peculiar essay, for right here where you would normally expect those alpine Conclusions, some Advice, some Stern Instructions & Directions, there's only the quiet murmur of the writer tiptoeing back to the story he or she was telling you in the second and third paragraphs. The story slips back into view gently, a little shy, holding its hat, nothing melodramatic, in fact it offers a few gnomic questions without answers, and then it gently slides away off the page and off the stage, it almost evanesces or dissolves, and it's only later, after you have read the essay three

87

times with mounting amazement, that you see quite how the writer managed the stagecraft there, but that's the stuff of another essay for another time.

And finally the last paragraph. It turns out that the perfect nature essay is quite short, it's a lean taut thing, an arrow and not a cannon. and here at the end there's a flash of humor, and a hint or tone or subtext of sadness, a touch of rue, you can't quite put your finger on it but it's there, a dark thread in the fabric, and there's also a shot of espresso hope, hope against all odds and sense, but rivetingly there's no call to arms, no clarion brassy trumpet blast, no website to which you are directed, no hint that you, yes you, should be ashamed of how much water you use or the car you drive or the fact that you just turned the thermostat up to seventy, or that you actually have not voted in the past two elections despite what you told the kids and the goat. Nor is there a rimshot ending, a bang, a last twist of the dagger. Oddly, sweetly, the essay just ends with a feeling eerily like a warm hand brushed against your cheek, and you sit there, near tears, smiling, and then you stand up. Changed.

CHRIS ALLING
Departure
From ENGS 1, Spring 2011

It begins softly. Just a few piano notes plodding through a steady rhythm above a barely-heard rustling that shuffles out of the mix like the last visitor leaving a hospital room. There is weight in these sounds, a mournful atmosphere drenched in regret and solemnity. The listener becomes hypnotized as the notes hang in the still air with moribund resonance. Each pressing of the piano keys tugs at the soul with enough force to suggest that the player is trying to communicate *something*. But the words of a single, plaintive voice interrupting the monotonous cadence penetrate one's being to implant a fully-formed idea that music alone cannot express.

And so it is that lyrical content arises as the most critical component of Radiohead's "Videotape," an ominous and genuinely sad outro to their album *In Rainbows*. This fact may seem erroneous given that singer Thom Yorke allows the listener to traverse much of the aural landscape of the song without his accompaniment. Sparseness, however, is critical to the effectiveness of this piece. The message of the lyrics might be diluted and undermined if too much language were present. Therefore, the careful selection of words and phrases confers the song with highly concentrated emotional and intellectual value. But this stylistic choice has no importance or function if there is no message to communicate. What, then, is Radiohead trying to convey through this composition? Careful analysis of the lyrics and the music that envelops them indicates that "Videotape" is actually a critique of social technology and its effect on human interaction. The packaging of this underlying theme within the context of a rather simple song is what ultimately makes this piece intriguing and altogether convincing.

Consider Yorke's opening line: "When I'm at the pearly gates ..." The theme of death (or, at least, finality) is immediately established, suggesting that "The End" is near. Nevertheless, there is a sense of hope in these words, optimism that the termination of one era will be met with the promise of another in Heaven. The next couplet of lines pushes the balance of emotions back towards anxiety with the words, "Mephistopheles is just beneath / And he's reaching out to grab me." This statement is referring to Johann Goethe's epic *Faust* in which the demon Mephistopheles comes to Earth to collect the protagonist's soul; the evocation of his very name expresses the ubiquity and inescapability of death in everyday life. In this way, one is able to see the two forces of Good and Evil juxtaposed together as they vie for Yorke's future.

Additionally, the use of the *Faust* reference expresses a certain amount of respect for the listener that further engages him or her within the dialogue of the song. Yorke is expecting that his audience is already familiar with the exploits of Mephistopheles or, if not, that they will perform their own research to uncover the meaning behind his words. Utilizing such a literary device empowers the listener with a sense of accomplishment and forges an intellectual connection strengthened by active, rather than passive, listening. The audience consequently *cares* about Yorke's fate as he is suspended in a metaphysical realm between eternal happiness and damnation. Mephistopheles plays only a figurative role in this struggle, however, necessitating the identification of the true force obstructing his passage into Heaven.

The culprit remains anonymous until the pivotal third stanza, where the blame is not directed at a tangible person or object but towards a more amorphous and abstract entity. Specifically, the repetition of "in red, blue, green" marks the most effective rhetorical strategy invoked by Radiohead in the entire song, for its functionality does not exist on a single plane but rather reaches multiple dimensions.

It is in this line that technology is first identified and personified as a villain. Red, blue and green are the three primary colors of light from which all other shades and tones are generated by technological displays. Of course, the human brain only perceives other colors by assimilating combinations of these three wavelengths of light detected by the cone cells of the eye. However, conscious associations between specific mixtures of the primary colors and the complementary colors that they create generally do not occur in the mind. For example, the thought of "yellow" does not immediately correspond to the thought of "green and blue blended together." But computers do perceive color in this way, and consequently they must distill all of the yellows and magentas and cyans of the universe to a collection of mixtures with no distinct identity or emotional value of their own. The simplification of the images on Yorke's "videotape" to this rudimentary color palette demonstrates that he no longer perceives the world from an organic perspective, that his aesthetic sensibilities have been reduced to that of a machine.

Yorke's mode of vocal delivery has been affected as well. The repetition he employs in this line reflects the detrimental influence that many technologies exact on unsuspecting minds. The droning pace, the stunted range of notes, the subtle wavering and fading of his voice: it seems as though Yorke is not willing himself to sing the words but rather is carrying out the demands of the music that surrounds him. Indeed, he sounds brainwashed into absent-minded subservience. Correspondingly, a television or computer can have the same sort of effect on its user. Eyes glaze over and facial muscles relax into a vacant expression as all connections to the exterior world are cut loose. The user then lives out his or her existence in a fog of detachment and apathy. Many people have already fallen prey to this trap, and through simulating their behavior Yorke attempts to warn the unaffected of the doom that they will face should they decide to give themselves fully to technology.

Perhaps the scariest implications for future technological innovation lie within the realm of interpersonal interaction. Social networking sites have substantially increased the ways in which people can interact and in doing so have created a generation of humans that need not rely on direct, physical communication to contribute to society. Yorke finds himself victim to this syndrome as he laments, "This is my way of saying goodbye / Because I can't do it face to face." This line encapsulates the role of social media as a defense system, a form of protection from difficult situations that might otherwise become complicated or painful if conducted in person. Dependence upon technology as a communication tool thereby strips the soul of all its resolve and makes it weak; such fragility is manifested in Yorke's voice, which reverberates as though his vocal cords are in danger of withering away. The overall effect is the reduction of the human voice to something less, ironically conferring more power to technology as it seeks to usurp its creator.

Irony and contrast carry over into the end of the song as Radiohead expresses serious doubts about humanity's ability to escape this unfortunate decline into technology-induced weakness. The final lines express the lone indication of contentment within the song and are included only to indicate Yorke's thankfulness for his imminent demise. With his statement, "Today [referring to the day of his 'death'] has been the most perfect day I've ever seen," he basks in the glory of his departure from a world plagued by impersonality, loneliness and disillusion. For the listener, it is a bittersweet departure; Yorke has finally found happiness but cannot share it with his audience. Instead, a bleak outlook diffuses from his words, a feeling that mankind's days shall only grow darker as handshakes, hugs, smiles and shared laughter are forever eradicated from the human vocabulary. The selfishness with which he guards his bliss only serves as another symptom of technology's deleterious influence on emotion. Consequently, little sympathy for the condition of his exit remains as his voice fades away, leaving behind a mechanical composition littered with metallic clipping and eerie rattling. This is the place that he has left behind, a wasteland of noises whirring above the lonesome, wistful notes of the piano. And in these notes remains some shred of humanity. But soon, they too are gone.

PROJECT 4

Extending the Inquiry

JENNY EVERETT
My Little Brother on Drugs
From *Popular Science*

I swipe an alcohol-soaked gauze pad over my younger brother's left thigh, an inch below the hem of his SpongeBob boxers. As I screw the needle into the injection pen, Alex feeds me instructions. It's my first time, but already it's his thirty-seventh.

"Here are the rules: insert the needle quickly and gently, but only when I say so," he says, taking the pen to pantomime the motion. He removes the first of two protective caps and turns a knob on the pen — one, two, three, four, five clicks — and watches intensely as his dose is released into the barrel.

"Make sure the skin dimples. That means the needle is all the way in," he continues. "Press the button until it clicks, then hold it there for five seconds. Keep the skin dimpled, otherwise all the medicine won't go in me. When you take out the needle, do it straight up and fast. And, Jenny, please don't hit a vein. That *huwts* me." Suddenly, dropping his *r*, Alex sounds much more like his nine-year-old self.

I pinch a clump of skin between my thumb and index finger and wait. "OK," he whispers. But I can't do it. "*OK*," he repeats. I pierce the fatty tissue and wince — and take it as a compliment that he doesn't. "Keep dimpling!" he yells.

Here's the thing: my brother isn't sick. He's short. Shorter than every boy and girl in Ms. Lemcke's fourth-grade class, shorter than 97 percent of boys his age. What I've just shot into his 3-feet-11¾-inch, fifty-pound body is Humatrope, a lab-brewed human growth hormone (hGH) nearly identical to the hGH secreted by the pituitary gland, the critical metabolic hormone that regulates not only height, as its name suggests, but also cardiac function, fat metabolism, and muscle growth.

Alex's quest for "enheightenment," as I've come to call it, began last summer just as the Food and Drug Administration expanded its approved uses of Humatrope, Eli Lilly and Company's recombinant hGH, to include children of idiopathic short stature (ISS) — kids who are extremely short for reasons that are not entirely understood. Kids who, like Alex, are teased or ignored by classmates who may trump their height by a foot — but whose "condition" may be caused by nothing more than genetics. This groundbreaking and controversial FDA ruling made Humatrope available to 400,000 American children expected to grow no taller than 5 feet 3 in the case of boys and 4 feet 11 in the case of girls, putting them in the bottom 1.2 percent. For Alex, the nightly hGH shots will probably continue for six to eight years — all to make this otherwise healthy boy grow taller.

Human growth is an invisible but intense process, an intricate and little understood web of genes, hormones, and other variables. Genetics aside, growth hormone may be the single biggest player. Between ten and thirty times a day, your hypothalamus sends a growth hormone-releasing hormone to the garbanzo-beans-size pituitary gland at the base of your brain. Each time the pituitary gland receives a signal, it spits out a small amount of growth hormone. Although scientists think a small percentage of hGH travels to your bones, a majority of the hormone latches onto binding proteins, which carry it to receptors in your liver cells. This triggers the secretion of insulin-like growth factor-1 (IGF-1), a protein that promotes bone growth in children and teenagers until their growth plates, areas at the ends of the bones, fuse, at around age seventeen for boys or fifteen for girls. After that, growth hormone continues to regulate the metabolic system, burning fat and building muscle, but we produce exponentially less by hGH each decade after puberty. Thus the teenager who can routinely "supersize it" without consequence ages into the thirty-year-old whose beer and burgers go straight to his gut.

In 1971, Berkeley chemist Choh Hao Li synthesized the growth hormone molecule, an enormous biotech breakthrough, and in 1985 synthetic growth hormone was approved by the FDA to treat growth hormone deficiency. Prior to the drug's development, medicinal growth hormone was scarce. What did exist had to be extracted from the pituitary glands of human corpses — most of the time legally, but occasionally by pathologists being paid by suppliers to remove the hormone without permission from the deceased's family. As a result of the shortage, hGH treatment was conservative, reserved for kids who made very little if any growth hormone themselves. Between 1963 and 1985, 7,700 patients in the United States took the hormone. Ultimately, 26 of these patients died of Creutzfeldt-Jakob disease (CJD); the fatal brain disease that is similar to mad cow is thought to have contaminated a batch of the pituitary hormone doled out in the sixties and seventies. The FDA banned growth hormone when the first two case of CJD were reported in early 1985 — just in time for the agency's approval, later that year, of the synthetic version.

Suddenly, the growth hormone supply was unlimited, safer, and less expensive, opening the door for looser diagnoses, along with higher and more frequent doses. By 1988 what had once been a niche drug prescribed to treat dwarfism was shattering all market expectations, chalking up more than a half billion dollars in annual sales.

At the time, I was eleven years old and a ripe candidate for growth hormone supplementation. I had been born in the fifth percentile for height, but at age five my "growth velocity" started slipping, and by eleven, I was hovering below the first percentile. Blood tests revealed that I was producing only "borderline acceptable" levels of growth hormone. "Growth hormone injections may be an option," Yale pediatric endocrinologist William Tamborlane told my parents. The prospect terrified me. "I don't care if I'm a midget! It's what's inside that counts!" I protested. "I'm not having a shot every day."

Further testing showed that my thyroid gland was malfunctioning, a definable and common condition called hypothyroidism. Tamborlane prescribed a pill (which I will take every day for the rest of my life), and my growth velocity picked up immediately. Still, I was told that I would never surmount the magical 5-foot threshold.

That's because most short children can place primary blame for their stature on the genetic lottery. "Want to be taller, Jenny?" I remember Tamborlane asking me as his eyes shifted between my slumping growth chart, my X-rays, and my mom and dad. I nodded eagerly. "Well, you should've picked different parents." He chuckled, while I considered the merits of a parentectomy. Today I'm twenty-six years old and my height has topped off at . . . 5 feet 1, thank you very much.

Fifteen years after I flirted with growth hormone treatment, biotech's baby has exploded into a $1.5 billion industry that has reached more than 200,000 children and sent many more to the doctor wondering if hGH is for them — including my brother Alex. When my mom called to tell me Alex was growth-hormone-deficient and would soon begin injections, I was skeptical. The prospect of having a shot every day had sent fear through my own little body, and now, as an overprotective big sister, I didn't want my brother's carefree childhood to be interrupted by such stress — and such a serious, understudied medical treatment — unless it was entirely necessary. Is being short so horrible that it should be medicalized and treated as an illness?

My thoughts were interrupted by my mom's voice, bringing me back to reality. "Nurses are coming over next week to show us how to administer the injection," she said. The decision had been made.

As the no. 6 squeals under Manhattan's Upper East Side, Alex's Nikes sway 3 inches above the floor. My brother is a happy kid whose sprite profile doesn't resemble that of the typical round-faced growth-hormone-deficient cherub. He's silent now, but only because his mouth is full of jelly beans. The train reaches our stop, and Alex places his sticky little hand in mine.

"Excuse me," he says politely as we jostle our way off.

A surprised middle-aged mom looks up from her book. "My, you are much more polite than *my* kindergartener," she says.

It's been about two weeks since Alex began his nightly injections. Before that, he might have flinched at this well-intentioned under-estimate of his age. But today he squares himself a bit and responds with a certain pride: "I'm nine years old," he says, "and I'm on Humatrope!"

It strikes me, not for the first time, just how important the drug has become to Alex. He yearns to be taller. As the youngest of six, he knows how to get noticed — our family joke is that he swallowed an amplifier — and what he lacks in stature he was dealt in personality. But at school, where tall kids hold the social scepter, his big personality is overlooked.

"Everyone says that it's what's inside that counts, and that makes me feel good," Alex says, "but if I was the tallest instead of the shortest, everything would just be better. People would sit with me at lunch, I'd have more friends, and people in my class wouldn't make fun of me and call me Little Everett. And I'd be a better soccer goalie. I think 6 feet would be good."

Studies show that half of short kids report being teased and three-quarters say they're treated as younger than their age — but keep in mind that this is an awkward age to begin with. Starting at about age ten, grade-wide height discrepancies tend to widen dramatically, which just adds to the broader stew of middle-school insecurities that most of us shudder to recall. This is the age at which families often become conscious of and concerned about growth issues — because discrepancies are suddenly so visually apparent.

When I was in the fifth grade, the boys would chase me down the hall on their knees playing "catch the midget," and one of the tougher girls would taunt me: "You're so small I need a microscope to see you." But before feeling sorry for me, consider my classmate Kelly (her name has been changed), who was 5 feet 10, a full 2 feet taller than I was — a virtual fifth-grade giant. (Given social norms, it's appropriate to compare the experience of being a short boy to that of being a tall girl.) Kelly was tortured so badly throughout adolescence that at eighteen she became bulimic. When her weight dropped to 115 pounds, she was hospitalized. "I thought it would make me smaller and more attractive," she recalled in a recent phone conversation. "It almost killed me."

Being a tall girl is so psychologically traumatic, in fact, that in the 1950s, doctors began giving tall girls estrogen as a growth suppressant. In high doses, the hormone stimulates cartilage maturation without causing an increase in height, which means the girls stop growing earlier. In Kelly's case, treatment was discussed, but doctors were confident, based on her bone development, that she wouldn't grow much taller than 6 feet. Good call: today Kelly is only an inch taller than she was in fifth grade. And although no formal long-term studies have been done, tall girls treated with estrogen have reported increased incidences of miscarriage, endometriosis, infertility, and ovarian cysts. Yet a survey taken last year reported that one-third of pediatric endocrinologists have offered the treatment at least once in the past five years.

Learning about the side effects of estrogen therapy only increased my apprehension about treating Alex with hGH. Armed with a small forest of research, I drove up to Yale-New Haven Children's Hospital to unload my worries on Dr. Myron Genel, Alex's pediatric endocrinologist.

With his white hair and white lab coat, Genel looks like the prototypical old-school doctor, the kind you imagine making house calls with his little black medical kit. I take a sip of my coffee. "This won't stunt my growth, will it?" I joke. "Too late to worry about that," he replies.

I reach into my bag and pull out binders of research: diagrams of the growth process, historical time lines, and a folder labeled "risk," which is packed with studies. "How concerned should my family be about the risks?" I ask.

I wait for reassurance — or, in any case, for a defense of Alex's treatment. But Genel surprises me.

"We honestly don't know the long-term side effects, and I think that's a reason for real concern," he says. "We're using a hormone that promotes growth, and there are things whose growth we don't want to promote. IGF-1, for example, has been shown to play a role in the development of malignancies in tissue culture."

This I knew. Multiple studies of human serum specimens have shown that elevated levels of IGF-1 identify people at higher risk for developing breast, prostate, and colon cancer, and tumor specimens, most studies show, have more IGF-1 receptors than normal adjacent cells. Although it's not yet known whether an abundance of IGF-1 actually causes malignancies or is merely associated with some other risk factor, it is a reason for concern because growth hormone is what stimulates the liver and tissues to produce IGF-1.

But Genel explains that he'll test Alex's IGF levels every three months to make sure they're in what's considered the normal range. "In theory, if we keep his growth factors at an acceptable level, he's not at risk," he says.

I scan my list of questions, typed up in order of progressing intensity, and zoom to the bottom. "Given the risks, what makes Alex a good candidate?"

Again his response surprises me — this time because it challenges my assumption that Alex is in fact a good candidate for treatment. "We can define those youngsters who make virtually no growth hormone, because they have a very typical presentation," he says. "And we can generally sort out those youngsters who make an ample amount of growth hormone. We have a very difficult time, however, defining youngsters like your brother, who make some growth hormone, but who possibly don't make enough."

He explains that although Alex's levels of IGF-1 are low and his height has gradually declined to the first percentile, he does produce *some* growth hormone.

"Your brother is a murky case, and there are enough questions about the safety and efficacy of this drug that I cannot say one way or another whether he should definitely receive treatment," he continues. "Frankly, I felt we could wait — but not very much longer — and gather information. It was a decision that your family made and, I suspect, Alex made."

Here is a manifestation of just how complicated and unpredictable the growth process is: it's impossible to measure hGH levels using a simple blood test. Because the hormone oscillates in the blood, constantly peaking and sinking, a hundred samples can yield a hundred different answers. So doctors must rely on growth hormone stimulation tests, where the patient is injected with an artificial agent that stimulates the pituitary gland to produce growth hormone. After the agent is injected, nurses sample the patient's blood every thirty minutes for two hours, hoping to catch the pituitary operating at full strength.

"These are artificial tests," Genel says. "None of them tell us anything about what a youngster does under normal circumstances. It only tells us that if you give them an artificial stimulus, the pituitary gland will release hormone."

Genel shows me my brother's test results: Alex produced readings ranging from 0.11 to 9.9 ng/ml. Though most doctors look for a top level of at least 10 as an indicator of healthy hormone production, Yale has a lower benchmark of 7 or greater. So by Yale's standards, Alex passed. My parents, I realize, have no idea that Alex may not be growth-hormone-deficient by some careful definition; they believe he is clinically deficient. Essentially my little brother is an experiment.

Over dinner that night, my mother and father recall the day Alex's test results arrived in the mail. Startled by the low numbers, they assumed he was producing far too little growth hormone. They had no idea growth hormone production is so difficult to measure. "I'm a parent, not a scientist," my mom says. "I shouldn't have to know that." It's safe to take him off the drug, I tell them: "It's not too late to change your mind."

But despite the day's revelations, they decide to move forward with treatment. Alex's confidence has already soared since starting Humatrope; they don't have the heart to disappoint him. Besides, my parents say, they're concerned Alex will have fewer professional opportunities, and they worry he won't find a woman to be with, if his height remains in the basement.

Such anxieties, of course, are hardly unique to my parents — and, in fact, a quick glance at the research would appear to back them up. A recent University of Florida study, for example, found that each extra inch of height amounted to $789 more a year in pay. So someone who is 6 feet would be expected, on average, to earn $5,523 more annually than someone who is 5 feet 5. Another study indicates that just 3 percent of Fortune 500 CEOs are shorter than 5 feet 7, and more than half are taller than 6 feet, though only 20 percent of the population is.

But it's not as simple an equation as these numbers make it seem, says Dr. David Sandberg, an associate professor of psychiatry and pediatrics at the University of Buffalo. Sandberg's studies have found that although short kids are teased and treated as younger than their age, there is no evidence that making them 2½ inches taller will make any difference in their quality of life. "Our lives are so much more complicated than one single factor," Sandberg says.

In clinical trials by Humatrope manufacturer Eli Lilly, children taking the drug grew on average 1 to 1½ inches more than the placebo group; 62 percent of the kids tested grew more than 2 inches over their predicted adult height, and 31 percent gained more than 4 inches. This would land Alex, whose predicted height without growth hormone is about 5 feet 6, somewhere between 5 feet 7 and 5 feet 10.

Dr. Harvey Guyda, chair of the department of pediatrics at McGill University in Canada, questions the studies, especially given what he describes as a high dropout rate. In the Eli Lilly studies, he points out, only 28 percent of the placebo and 42 percent of the growth hormone-therapy subjects completed the study; it seems reasonable to assume, he says, that the subjects who endured the study were the ones who demonstrated the most extreme growth.

"The mantra is that healthy, short kids are handicapped, abnormal, have all sort of problems, and we have to do something," says Guyda, who testified against the FDA's approval of Humatrope for treating kids with ISS. "But there is no data to prove that these kids are any different from normal-stature children, and there is absolutely zero data that says when you give growth hormone to a kid who's said to have this psychosocial problem because he's short there's any benefit. Prove to me that a few extra inches is worth the cost of daily injections."

Financially alone, that cost, according to Guyda, amounts to $10,000 per centimeter for a growth hormone-deficient kid, and somewhere between $22,000 and $43,000 per centimeter for kids with idiopathic short stature. For now, my parents' insurance company, Anthem Blue Cross and Blue Shield, has agreed to cover Alex's treatment, but not every short child has insurance or a pediatric endocrinologist to recommend treatment. The not-surprising result is that any advantage hGH does confer will likely go to already advantaged patients: rich, white American males. (For every two girls who receive treatment, five boys do; this is at least partly explained by the fact that boys suffer more discrimination in relation to their short stature than girls do.)

A week before Alex's three-month checkup, I return to Yale, this time to meet with Tamborlane, my own pediatric endocrinologist, whom I haven't seen since my last appointment eight years ago. I'm especially interested in his opinion about Alex because Tamborlane, now the chief of pediatric endocrinology at Yale, voted for the approval of Humatrope to treat idiopathic short stature. We meet in the cafeteria, and although I'm not looking for a free checkup, he palpates my throat right there. "Thyroid feels healthy," he reports.

Tamborlane voted for the approval, he tells me, because the drug was already approved to treat some groups of children who produce plenty of growth hormone — children with Turner syndrome, a genetic abnormality; children born small for gestational age; and children with chronic renal insufficiency, a kidney disease. In each of these cases, hGH isn't treating the disease, it's treating the resulting undesirable physical characteristic-short stature. In kids with ISS, though, it's even more ambiguous because the disease, if there is one, is unknown.

I present Alex's case to Tamborlane, explaining my family's motivations and the uncertainty surrounding the diagnosis. I tell him that although I want Alex to have every advantage and the best possible quality of life, I'm concerned about the drug's unclear benefits and the potential long-term risks for kids who are short for reasons that aren't fully understood.

"If Alex were your son," I ask, "would you put him on hGH?"

Tamborlane leans back and pauses to consider the question.

"Given the uncertainties, probably not. I was a short, geeky kid at a football prep school, and I survived — maybe even gained something from it," he says. (He's now 5 feet 9.) "All signs say Alex would probably grow to a very livable height without the growth hormone."

In early November, we bring Alex to Yale for his first checkup. By now the injection has become routine — slotted into a nine P.M. Nickelodeon commercial break — and my family is already noticing changes in Alex's body. His muscle tone is visibly improved, and his pants are suddenly too short. In the waiting room, I jot down a few things to mention to the doctor: Alex's appetite is uncharacteristically voracious; his growth pains are intensifying; and his hair is dry and brittle.

The room used for measuring height and weight is wallpapered with drawings by patients with a variety of metabolic disorders. One depicts a small, sad-looking stick figure labeled "before" and a taller, much happier stick figure labeled "after." Alex stands to the left of this, his back to the wall, grinning in anticipation of his "after." The nurse scribbles on his chart and ushers us into the examining room. Alex is anxious because while we swear he's grown at least 3 inches, we're not positive because we haven't measured him yet — psychologists recommend we don't measure Alex at home.

Finally Genel announces, "124.8 cm. That's just about 4 feet 1, about an inch and a half in three months."

"Wow," says my mom, extrapolating 6 inches of growth a year.

"That's *all?*" says Alex. "All those shots for one measly inch?!"

Genel warns them not to take the results too literally. "These are *positive* results," he says to Alex. Then, turning to my mom: "But it's too early attribute this response to the treatment."

Indeed, there's no telling what the results of Alex's treatment will be; even at $20,000 a year there are no guarantees. Some kids end up in sixtieth percentile, while others never crawl above the fifth. I'm still left wondering why we're rolling the dice on a healthy kid, particularly when the benefits of a few extra inches are unproven and the risks are unknown. At the same time, I'm rooting for results — and we leave the doctor's office cautiously optimistic that the treatment is having an impact. We're further reassured three months later, in early February, when Alex's next official measurement comes in: He's 4 feet 2½ inches, a full 2½ inches taller than he was six months earlier when he began treatment.

HANNAH PRESCOTT
Holding the Pieces Together
From ENGS 104, Fall 2010

If you are the type of person who asks the older man who has been staring at the same grocery store shelf for 20 minutes whether he needs help finding anything or who waits patiently while he struggles to think of the right word when answering you, I would like to thank you. Because that kind, older man who cannot remember what he was looking for is someone to somebody out there, who loves him and worries about him. That patient, generous man who hesitates before recalling the correct word is someone's friend, brother, and father, who is sick and will never get better. That man . . . is my grandfather.

Of my two grandparents, my grandmother was always the organized one. She was one who made the plans, sent the bills in on time, remembered birthdays, holidays, appointments, people's names (and everything about them, too). She loved people, and she loved my grandfather. And they fit together perfectly.

From what I can remember, they were never really apart. They weren't the kind of people who realize they desire something different out of life or who begin to value their independence over each other's company after decades together. They were old New Englanders: loyal to the core, unbreakable, inseparable.

But then she died.

Suddenly, my grandfather was left completely alone in the house in which they had made their life for more than 40 years. After her death, no one was surprised when my grandfather was struggling — my grandmother was irreplaceable.

Without her, my grandfather had trouble with common things; he misplaced items, often stopped chores half-finished, forgot words — sometimes forgot people — and had difficulty with manual skills he had excelled at his entire life. We thought we understood why. He had never had to be completely in charge and responsible for remembering everything before. He was the dairy farmer-soldier-car mechanic-carpenter-house painter who was suddenly thrust into a situation where he was overloaded with loneliness, grief, and wanting to remember everything his wife had been able to do effortlessly.

As time went on, my grandfather continued to struggle. His natural relaxed pace of talking slowed even more as he paused to recall words and facts that had been on the tip of his tongue only moments before. Usually a cautious and meticulous worker, he almost electrocuted himself when he forgot to turn off the electricity before starting to fix our dishwasher. We thought that his forgetfulness and confusion were just a part of getting older. But then the Alzheimer's that had been lurking in his brain revealed itself, and we realized all of the changes and struggles he had experienced for years weren't solely caused by age or grief. He was sick and we hadn't been able to put all the pieces together quick enough.

Alzheimer's is a lonely, difficult, heart-breaking disease that, according to the Alzheimer Association website, presently affects 5.3 million Americans. A type of dementia, the disease affects the brain starting with the part responsible for memory. As the disease progresses, a brain affected by Alzheimer's functions less and less normally. All of the changes occurring in the brain are reflected in the changes of a family member's personality or behavior, which the Family Caregiver Alliance website acknowledges can be very challenging for a family to cope with. For my family, my grandfather's new tendency to automatically view situations negatively is extremely stressful. Previously an easy-going optimist, he now focuses on problems he finds in a situation, whether it's slightly higher gas prices or the "poor" service at a restaurant we have enjoyed eating at for years. This behavior is so unlike him that it's immediately obvious to us. My grandfather, like all Alzheimer patients, is fading away from the person that he used to be an "inch at a time"; a phrase used by Professor Cowan, a sociology professor at UVM and an expert on aging, to describe the process of change.

All of the changes that the family member with Alzheimer's is undergoing affect those close to them. This is especially true because relatives usually function as the primary caregivers, as is the case with my family. While people prefer to be cared for by their family, having a family member as a caregiver can be difficult because it alters the relationships that people have spent decades developing, a topic discussed in the book *Taking Care of Aging Family Members: A Practical Guide* by Wendy Lustbader and Nancy Hooyman.

This role change that occurs between family members is an issue, especially when children are caregivers to their sick parents. A child, even one who is grown up, is used to viewing her parent a certain way. Deborah Hoffman, the director of a documentary following her mother's experience with Alzheimer's titled *Complaints of a Dutiful Daughter*, which follows her mother's experience with Alzheimer's, had trouble dealing with her mother as the disease progressed. Her image of her mother drastically changed within a short time as the strong, intelligent woman she knew became fixated, confused, and antagonistic towards her. For Deborah Hoffman, the woman that she was taking care of was "not her mother," and coping with the change was difficult for her. "Children" caregivers, like Deborah Hoffman, are forced to cope with the high emotional stress of altered relationship roles with their relatives, who are simultaneously fading away from them.

As well as dealing with their own emotions about the changes caused by their relative's sickness, caregivers have to work to achieve a balance between keeping their family member safe and not controlling them. Since Alzheimer's impairs a person's judgment, Professor Cowan cautions that family members with the disease may behave in ways that create dangerous situations. Last winter, my grandfather, who is usually very careful and safe, ran over a plugged-in extension cord with a snow blower. Even though he damaged the snow blower and almost seriously injured himself, he still insisted on finishing plowing our driveway although it was no longer safe to do so. The fact that he uncharacteristically put himself in a dangerous situation, and then didn't remove himself from it when he had the chance, showed my family that we were going to have to make some changes in order to keep him safe.

Although achieving the balance between safety and independence is difficult, Professor Cowan believes that it can be done if caregivers practice "freedom within limits." With the freedom within limits method, caregivers create a safe boundary for their relatives, and then allow them complete freedom within that boundary. For my family, this meant that one of us made sure all extension cords were unplugged and out of the way before my grandfather started to snow blow. We made the environment around him as safe as we could, so that he was free to do what he wanted within it.

For us, the freedom within limits method works well, especially when dealing with issues like the snow blower situation. But for many caregivers the consequences of controlling, or not controlling, their relative's behavior can lead to feelings of guilt. When discussing this topic, Professor Cowan introduced a scenario: a caregiver has a family member who wanders, which is also called "sundowning." The caregiver is faced with the decision of keeping the relative safe and controlled, or allowing personal freedom. To keep her relative safe, the caregiver could lock the front door to prevent the relative from wandering. However, if she believes that autonomy is more important, she can leave the door unlocked and take the chance that her relative may wander. This is a common scenario caregivers face as indicated by the fact that the Alzheimer's Association website states that about 60% of people with Alzheimer's wander, and it also highlights the decisions with which caregivers are presented. Professor Cowan acknowledges that caregivers will approach the scenario differently, but says that it's important for caregivers to make sure they are able to deal and live with the consequences of their decisions, whatever they are.

The responsibility and effort required of a family caregiver are described by the National Institute on Aging website as having a "high physical, emotional, and financial" toll on the individual. The stress of caregiving can be heightened if there are issues that haven't been resolved yet between the patient, the caregiver, and any siblings who may also be in the picture. Unfortunately, this is very common, and Professor Cowan says that issues from the past may cause caregivers to be resentful of having to take care of their parent. Problems that siblings had before are only enhanced by the stressful situation, and often lead to unequal responsibility for the sick parent. Many siblings simply refuse to accept that their parent has Alzheimer's. *Taking Care of Aging Family Members: A Practical Guide* discusses that many "children" do nothing to help because they don't believe that there is an issue, leaving their siblings to do all the work.

The Family Caregiver Alliance website recommends that people who are experiencing stressful issues with their relatives "try to forgive family members [because] the only thing that [you] have control over in a situation is [your] own actions. Attempt to work through your negative emotions to take care of yourself and move forward." This may seem counterintuitive since, once again, it puts all the pressure on the primary caregiver to take care of, and take responsibility for, everything. But Professor Cowan's advice echoes the Alliance's opinion. Her take on the issue is that people can't fix their relatives — sick or healthy — no matter how hard they try. She adds that "self-healing doesn't require anything from the offender" and if a person is able to forgive, then she will be capable of caring for the sick relative completely and "unconditionally."

According to the Family Caregiver Alliance website, caregivers who are unable to do this, and others who are simply exhausted, experience what is known as "caregiver burnout." Feelings of duty and guilt can lead family members to invest all of their time in taking care of their sick relative. While this is done with the best intentions, it usually backfires because, as Professor Cowan puts it, "you cannot give what you do not have." Those who lack a support system, or who don't take care of themselves, simply wear down and wear out. There are many factors that influence caregiver burnout: the family's attitude toward the situation, how well the family can communicate with each other, the economic resources available, and the supportiveness of their spouse. Caregiver burnout has major consequences. The Family Caregiver Alliance website states that it "is one of the most-cited reasons for caregivers placing a loved one in a nursing home or other long-term care facility" — therefore, it is very important for caregivers to remember to take care of themselves, too.

The whole caretaking process is emotionally stressful — from finding out the diagnosis to thinking about nursing homes. Nursing homes can be incredibly expensive and have limited space. Families may prefer or be forced to take care of their family member at home, but the majority of families will reach the point when having a family member caretaker is no longer safe or beneficial. While doing so may be saddening, Professor Cowan recommends that caregivers start to prepare years in advance in case a crisis occurs. Just because caregivers put their relative on a waiting list for a nursing home doesn't mean that they have to use it, but it does allow for options.

While knowing that admitting a family member into a nursing home may be the best for the relative and the caregiver, it doesn't reduce the feeling of guilt that many experience. Deborah Hoffman states in her documentary that she "felt like [she] had just done the most horrible thing to a person that [she] could absolutely do" when she put her mother into a nursing home. While I know my own family may reach this point soon, I am not prepared for it. It will the best decision to let professionals take care of my grandfather in a safe setting when he gets worse, but no matter how I think about it, it still seems like we are going to be abandoning and giving up on him. It will seem like we didn't love him enough, even though I know it's not true. When addressed with this concern, Professor Cowan suggested that those who feel guilty should simply think about the situation differently: "Don't think of it as getting rid of responsibility; it's putting their needs first;" and it's just another way of making sure that they are safe.

For anyone who is taking care of a relative with Alzheimer's, don't be afraid to look for outside support. The Alzheimer's Association of Vermont and New Hampshire has education programs and support groups to help the family and caregiver understand the changes in their relative. The Champlain Valley Agency on Aging has an Alzheimer Caregiving Grant (that Professor Cowan helped develop), which gives a $2,000 grant to those who need caregiving relief, no strings attached.

Since many find that talking with others who are in the same situation is helpful, Professor Cowan recommends joining religious or support groups in your area. Also, don't hesitate to invest in things that make your life easier. For example, if a relative wanders, buy a GPS-tracker device that fits into the shoe so that you will always be able to find her, an idea that is discussed in Peggy Noonan's *USA Weekend* article, "Safety afoot, via GPS, for Alzheimer's patients".

One of the most helpful things that you can do is to educate yourself. You can instantly find specific and useful information online by checking out some of the websites below. They are a great place to start learning about Alzheimer's as a disease and about caregiving for a relative with Alzheimer's.

- The Alzheimer's Association: www.alz.org
- The National Institute on Aging: www.nia.nih.gov
- The Family Caregiver Alliance: National Center on Caregiving: www.caregiver.org

Finally, take some time to read *Taking Care of Aging Family Members: A Practical Guide* by Wendy Lustbader and Nancy Hooyman. It's written specifically for family caregivers and it full of helpful information, scenarios that you will relate with, and advice. Anyone who is taking care of a sick relative should follow the book's advice that by simply learning more about caregiving and the common issues that caregivers face everyday, the less alone and more capable you will feel.

DRAFT

If you are the type of person who asks the older man who has been staring at the same grocery store shelf for 20 minutes whether he needs help finding anything or who waits patiently while he tries to think of the right word when talking to you, I would like to thank you. Because that man is someone to somebody out there, who loves him and worries about him. That man is someone's friend, brother, and father, who is sick and will never get better. That man . . . is my grandpa.

Of my two grandparents, my grandma was always the organized one. She was one who made the plans, sent the bills in on time, remembered birthdays, holidays, appointments, people's names (and usually everything about them, too). She loved people, and she loved my grandpa. And they fit together perfectly. From what I can remember, they had never really been apart. They weren't the type of people who decided they want something different out of life after decades together, or start to value their independence over each other's company. They were old New Englanders: loyal to the core, unbreakable, inseparable.

But then she died.

Suddenly, my grandfather was left completely alone in the house they had made their life in for more than 40 years. When my grandfather was struggling, no one was surprised; my grandmother was irreplaceable.

Without her, my grandpa had trouble with common things; he misplaced items, often stopped chores half-finished, forgot words — sometimes forgot people — and had difficulty with manual skills he had excelled at his entire life. We thought we understood why. He had never had to be completely in charge or had to remember all these responsibilities before. He was the dairy farmer-soldier-car mechanic-carpenter-house painter suddenly thrust into a situation where he was overloaded with loneliness, grief, and wanting to remember everything his wife had been able to effortlessly.

He was changing, but the life around him, and us, was changing too. We thought that his forgetfulness and confusion was due to him becoming older. But then the Alzheimer's that had been lurking in his brain revealed itself, and we realized that we had missed something huge. We were the ones in the position to realize what exactly was wrong, and we hadn't been able to put all the pieces together quick enough.

Alzheimer's is a lonely, difficult, heart-breaking disease that presently affects 5.3 million Americans (8). Alzheimer's is a type of dementia that affects the brain, starting with the part responsible for memory (2). As the disease progresses, a brain affected by the disease functions less and less normally and the changes occurring in the brain are reflected in a family member's change in personality or behavior (10). Alzheimer's progresses in a way that is often referred as losing a person an "inch at a time", with a family member fading away from the person that they used to be (1).

All of the changes the family member with Alzheimer's experiences affect those close to them. This is especially true since relatives usually function as the primary caregiver (7). After receiving a difficult diagnosis, family caregivers are faced with learning new ways to work with the patient's dementia and memory loss in order to take care of them the best that they can (10).

While people prefer being cared for by family remembers (7), having a family member as a caregiver alters relationships. Role change is an issue, especially with older parents whose children are their caregivers. A child, even one that is grown up, is used to having viewed their parent through a certain lens

(1). Deborah Hoffman, the director of a documentary following her mother's experience with Alzheimer's titled Complaints of a Dutiful Daughter, had trouble dealing with her mother as the disease progressed. Her image of her mother drastically changed within a short time and, to her, the woman that she was taking care of was "not her mother" (6). "Children" caregivers are forced to deal with a lot as they experience changing relationship roles with their parent, who is gradually fading away from them at the same time.

Family caregivers face a myriad of issues when responsible for the welfare of a family member with Alzheimer's. While times may be difficult, Professor Brookes Cowan, a sociology professor at UVM and an expert on aging, says "the key to providing care for someone with Alzheimer's is to always think — what does the other person need?". It's necessary for a caregiver to always consider the patient's needs and to limit their own expectations (1).

Caregivers have to work to achieve a balance between not controlling their family member and keeping them safe. Since Alzheimer's impairs a person's judgment, they are likely to do dangerous things that they normally wouldn't (1). According to Prof. Cowan, the balance between constraint and freedom is termed "dignity with risk". By practicing dignity with risk, caregivers support the independence of the older person, even if their actions may result in dangerous consequences, but only if the person with Alzheimer's can understand the risks. This practice wouldn't work for everyone because it depends fully on the person's ability to make decisions and recognize consequences (1).

Caregivers can also find a balance by practicing "freedom within limits" (1). Caregivers will create a boundary for the family member with Alzheimer's and allow complete freedom within that boundary. But the consequences of controlling, and not controlling, behavior can lead to feelings of guilt. When discussing this topic, Cowan introduced a scenario: a caregiver has a family member who wanders (also called "sundowning"), and they are faced with the decision of keeping them safe and controlled, or allowing them personal freedom (1). This is a common scenario caregivers face since about 60% of people with Alzheimer's wander (8). The caregiver must decide if they should prevent the relative from wandering (by locking the front door, for example) or if they should take the chance that they might wander. Cowan acknowledges that different caregivers will approach the scenario differently, but says that regardless of their choice, caregivers should make sure that they are able to deal and live with the consequences of it (1).

The responsibility and effort that is required of a family caregiver takes a "high physical, emotional, and financial" toll on them (3). The stress of caregiving can be heightened if there are unresolved issues between the patient, the caregiver, and any siblings who may also be in the picture. Unfortunately, this is very common and unresolved issues may cause the caregiver to be resentful of having to take care of their parent (1). Also, unequal responsibility between siblings causes conflict as unsolved issues that siblings had before become enhanced by the stress caused by the situation. Many siblings refuse to accept that their parent has Alzheimer's and does nothing to help because they don't believe that there is an issue, leaving the other siblings to do all the work (7).

The Family Caregiving Association recommends that people who are experiencing stressful issues with their relatives "try to forgive family members ... [because] the only thing that we have control over in a situation is out own actions. Attempt to work through you negative emotions to take care of yourself and move forward" (4). This may seem counterintuitive since it, once again, puts all the pressure on the primary caregiver to take care, and take responsibility for everything. But Professor Cowan's advice echoes the association's opinion. Her take on the issue is that people can't fix their relatives — sick or healthy — no matter how hard they try. She adds that "self-healing doesn't require anything from the offender" and if a person is able to forgive, then they will be capable of caring for their sick relative completely and "unconditionally" (1).

Caregivers who are unable to do this, and others who are simply exhausted, experience what is known as "caregiver burnout" (5). People try to do too much but "you cannot give what you do not have" (1). There are many factors that can be looked at to see if someone will experience caregiver burnout: the family's attitude toward the situation, how well the family can communicate with each other, economic resources available, and how supportiveness of their spouse (1).

The whole caretaking process is emotionally stressful — from finding out the diagnosis to thinking about nursing homes. Nursing homes can be incredibly expensive, and have limited space. Families may prefer, or be forced to take care of their family member at home, but all will reach a point when having a family member caretaker is no longer safe or beneficial. While doing so may be depressing, Professor Cowan recommends that caregivers start to prepare years in advance in case a crisis occurs. Just because a caregiver puts their relative on a waiting list for a nursing home doesn't mean that they have to use it, but it does allow for options (1).

While knowing that putting a family member into a nursing home may be the best for the relative and the caregiver, it doesn't reduce the feeling of guilt that many experience. Deborah Hoffman stated in her documentary that she "felt like [she] had just done the most horrible thing to a person that [she] could absolutely do" when she dropped let her mother at a home (6). Although I know that my own family may reach this point soon, I am not prepared. It will the best decision to let professionals take care of my grandfather in safe setting when he gets worst, but no matter how I think about it, it still seems like we are going to be abandoning and giving up on him. It will seem like we didn't love him enough, even though I know it's not true. When addressed with this concern, Prof. Cowan said that for those who feel guilty, she suggests thinking about it differently: "Don't think of it as getting rid of responsibility; it's putting their needs first", and it's just another way of making sure that they are safe (1).

For anyone who is taking care of a relative with Alzheimer's, don't be afraid to look for outside support. The Alzheimer's Association for Vermont and New Hampshire has education programs and support groups to help the family and caregiver understand changes in their relative. The Champlain Valley Agency on Aging has an Alzheimer Caregiving Grant (that Prof. Cowan helped develop), which gives a $2,000 grant to those who need caregiving relief, no strings attached. Also, take some time to read Taking Care of Aging Family Members: A Practical Guide (7). It's written for caregivers and it full of helpful information, scenarios that you will relate with, and advice. Joining religious or local support groups can also be very helpful (1). Don't hesitate to invest in things that make your life easier. For example, if your relative wanders, buy a GPS-tracker device that fits into their shoe so that you will always be able to find them (9). The more you learn about caregiving and the common issues that caregivers deal with, the less alone and more capable you will feel (7).

SOURCES

1. Cowan, Brookes. Personal interview. 10 Oct. 2010.

2. "Alzheimer's Association — Facts and Figures." *Alzheimer's Association*. N.p., n.d. Web. 22 Sept. 2010. <http://www.alz.org/alzheimers_disease_facts_figures.asp>.

3. "Alzheimer's Disease Fact Sheet." *National Institute on Aging*. N.p., n.d. Web. 28 Sept. 2010. <http://www.nia.nih.gov/Alzheimers/Publications/adfact.htm>.

4. "Caregiving and sibling relationships: challenges and opportunities." *Family Caregiving Association*. N.p., n.d. Web. 28 Sept. 2010. \#60>www.caregiver.org/caregiver/jsp/content_node.jsp?nodeid=868>.

5. "Caring for Adults with Cognitive and Memory Impairment." *Family Caregiver Alliance*. N.p., n.d. Web. 10 Sept. 1928. <www.caregiver.org/caregiver/jsp/content_node.jsp?nodeid=392>.

6. *Complaints of a Dutiful Daughter*. Dir. Deborah Hoffmann. Perf. Deborah Hoffmann. PBS, 1994. VHS.

7. Lustbader, Wendy, and Nancy R. Hooyman. *Taking care of aging family members: a practical guide*. Rev. and expanded. ed. New York: Free Press ;, 1994. Print.

8. Maker, Jeff. "Alzheimer's Association — Local News." *Alzheimer's Association*. N.p., 22 Sept. 2010. Web. 8 Nov. 2010. <http://www.alz.org/vermont/in_my_community_news.asp>.

9. Noonan, Peggy. "Safety afoot, via GPS, for Alzheimer's patients." *Burlington Free Press* 17 Oct. 2010, sec. USA Weekend insert: 10. Print.

10. "Ten Real-Life Strategies for Dementia Caregiving." *Family Caregiving Alliance: National Center on Caregiving*. N.p., n.d. Web. 10 Sept. 1928. <www.caregiver.org/caregiver/jsp/content_node.jsp?nodeid=1134>.

STEPHANIE CESARIO

Are Suckers Breeding Suckers?

From ENGS 104, Fall 2010

If someone were to rummage through my purse, he or she would find a variety of objects, such as pens, books, and maybe some lip balm. The hidden secret though, often in a small pocket, is my self-diagnosed sweet tooth fix: the Tootsie Pop. Portable, delicious, affordable, and fat-free, Tootsie Pops help get me through boring classes and aid in cleansing the palette after a meal. A brief examination of the wrapper shows that the candy is largely composed of sugar, corn syrup, partially hydrogenated soybean oil, and soy lecithin, with some "artificial colors" thrown in for that cheery rainbow appeal. This did not sound particularly edible to me, even with that deliciously sweet taste; words like "lecithin" are more similar to a foreign language. American consumers like myself are generally clueless towards what they are ingesting, regularly glazing over vaguely labeled ingredients like "corn syrup" and "soy lecithin." This is not because of some oversight in the label production process; there has been a concerted effort throughout governmental and agricultural agencies to prevent detailed labeling of processed ingredients. This severe lack of transparency in the labeling of our snacks is mostly because companies involved in the production and sale of food do not want consumers to be deterred from purchasing an item if it is fully listed in its true form: as a molecularly enhanced chemical derived from genetic engineering. Almost all corn syrup, a sweetener, and soy lecithin, a preservative, are a result of genetically engineered seed, but the ingredient list fails to mention this at all. It is very disconcerting that I am eating genetically engineered, molecularly manipulated chemicals when enjoying a Tootsie Pop. Would you still purchase your favorite snack if it were clearly labeled as genetically engineered? Americans should be given the option to decide. It is time for consumers to educate themselves on what they are eating and advocate for clearly labeled ingredients.

Most Food and Drug Administration (FDA) labeling efforts thus far, along with the efforts of particular companies, are directed at clearer nutritional information. There has been a slight increase in the amount of information on packages that reveal the amount of calories and fat. While this is a positive improvement, it does not account for the lack of information regarding the actual risk of engineered sweeteners and preservatives that permeate our shelves. There are currently no labeling or safety regulations for genetically engineered foods in the United States, yet according to a recently published article in the science journal *Five Elements Press*, it is estimated that "nearly two thirds of all foods in U.S supermarkets may now be genetically modified." Most corn and soy-derived ingredients in processed snacks come from genetically modified seed specifically designed by the massive agribusiness Monsanto so that the crops are resistant to pesticides with which they are sprayed.

But it is still illegal in the U.S. to label an ingredient as "GM" or "GMO." The U.S. has actually tried to fight any form of international labeling and claimed that it is an infringement on free trade, proving especially resistant to the European Union's passing of strict labeling standards in 2002. The international organization Greenpeace states that it is "highly unfortunate that countries which choose to inform consumers about GE [genetically engineered] ingredients face opposition from the major producers of GE crops," specifically the US, which according to Greenpeace is one of the largest producers of GM crops in the world. Countries across the globe, such as Japan, China, Australia, and New Zealand, are outlawing GMOs, or requiring strict labeling. Even developing countries like Haiti, Nicaragua, Zimbabwe, and many others have rejected food aid from the U.S. because of its genetically engineered ingredients. But the FDA has not created any form of a cohesive policy concerning the labeling genetically modified ingredients. According to the investigative environmental news site *The Raw Story*, in the U.S., even if a product does not contain a processed, genetically engineered ingredient, the company cannot label it as such for fear that it will "confuse the consumer" into choosing a product based on false preconceptions of GMOs.

This governmental resistance to consumer awareness around GMOs is largely due to the tight connections between large biotech agriculture corporations, specifically Monsanto, and the food administrators at the top levels of policy-making. The Edmonds Institute and the Center for Responsive Politics released reports detailing the "revolving door" effect of government regulators, once retired, getting offered lucrative positions at the companies they had originally been regulating. According to the Edmonds Institute, a former laboratory supervisor for Monsanto is now a director of food safety in the FDA; an administrator in the U.S. Environmental Protection Agency is also the Vice President of Public Affairs for Monsanto, and the list continues. It is no wonder that there has been no progress made in labeling policies when the companies who are fighting the labeling have employees throughout U.S. governmental agencies.

Governmental agencies are additionally hesitant to the clear labeling of biotech ingredients because of their undying support of the production and distribution of high fructose corn syrup. The ever-controversial sweetener is present in a large portion of our food, and we generally accept it without questioning its affects on our bodies and the environment. As Michael Pollan discusses at the start of his best-selling book, *The Omnivore's Dilemma*, "The great edifice of variety and choice that is an American supermarket turns out to rest on a remarkably narrow biological foundation comprised of a tiny group of plants that is dominated by a single species: *Zea mays*, the giant tropical grass most Americans know as corn." While the variety of products, like Tootsie

Pops, seem to be vastly different, most come down to genetic manipulations of the same plant. Even the companies like ConAgra, who produce corn syrup, explain that it is mostly from genetically engineered corn, but that most corn syrup barely has any engineered corn DNA left in because it has gone through so much processing. Most varieties of the syrup, as detailed by the *Washington Posts* study, are derived from a molecular rearrangement of enzymes, resulting in an amped up fructose content. The study also found that more than half of the corn syrup varieties tested contained mercury, an element that, in high quantities, is toxic. The *American Journal of Clinical Nutrition* claims that average Americans have at least 120 calories of corn syrup per day, accumulating to nearly sixty pounds per year, so it is necessary to examine the direct affects. Unfortunately though, because corporations like Monsanto and ConAgra have patented their genetically engineered syrup product, research into detrimental health affects has been retarded, often through lawsuits. The cycle is continued through the governmental support of these companies when such research issues are brought to court.

According to the Institute for Responsible Technology (IRT), this lack of research becomes a major health issue for consumers, because engineering corn plants can create hundreds or even thousands of unknown DNA mutations, expressing genes in ways that have great potential to be detrimental to ecosystems and to health. Monsanto's infamous Bt corn, resistant to their RoundUp Ready pesticide, is claimed by the IRT to have been correlated with respiratory disease in field workers all over the world when the plants are shedding pollen. These hazards are not just limited to humans though; the Institute also cites the statistic that "more than 20 farmers in North America report that pigs fed GM corn varieties had low conception rates, false pregnancies, or gave birth to bags of water," with many forms of farm animals becoming sterile because of high contact with the ingredient. While it is impossible to fully track the health effects of such new technology yet, U.S. agencies are completely avoiding the precautionary principle, which according to University of Vermont Environmental Studies Department Chair Stephanie Kaza is the theory that new technology involving public and environmental health should be viewed as a threat until proven safe. In addition to these animal and human health issues with genetic corn syrup production, vast fields of high-yielding GM corn are tearing up ecosystems and stripping fertile soil across the U.S. Midwest. Yet governmental actors are treating the GMO as innocent until proven guilty. We are just beginning to become cognizant of some of the repercussions of all this DNA-manipulated corn, yet we grow and consume it more freely than almost any other food source.

While corn domineers our favorite snack foods, it is almost overshadowed by the other major culprit of processing and genetic engineering on our ingredient list: soybeans. Encompassed within "soy lecithin," soybeans are the largest GMO crop; *Five Elements Press* claims that over 75% of the U.S.'s current soybean crop is genetically modified. These two ingredients mostly act as emulsifying agents for a variety of candies beyond just the sweet suckers. The processed forms of engineered soybeans often are the most ambiguous items on an ingredient, but have been researched to have some of the most direct health affects. The IRT claims that laboratory experiments feeding mice GM soybeans have resulted in irregular cell shapes in the animals' liver and pancreas, sterility, and enzyme disruption. The real problem is that because these mutated seeds are patented by companies like Monsanto, most labs cannot even research their affects legally, so there has been a very limited amount of information released regarding their affects on mutating genes. The biggest evidence of foul play with these manipulated beans are the amount of allergies and allergic reactions popping up in humans, both those that work with the crop and ingest the crop. According to Schlosser in his best-selling book, an allergic reaction is the immune system's way of responding to something it deems foreign, so engineered varieties of crops like soybeans often spur these negative reactions.

Clearly, the Tootsie Pop label is missing some important information. While I do not expect a candy wrapper to contain all the health risks involved, American eaters deserve to know more without having to take time to thoroughly research it. There is a blatant veil between companies and consumers, leaving consumers to ingest unknown substances approved by an organization (the FDA) that is partially administered by the same people creating and selling the products. This web seems impenetrable and overwhelming because clearly the lack of transparency in a product's ingredients is not solved by a one-time solution. There are many factors involved, mostly surrounding corporate greed and a lack of general awareness, that allow for mysterious products to be sold and consumed freely. It may seem like ignorance truly is bliss when it comes to such a personal, necessary aspect of life as food. Can't I just enjoy my Tootsie Pop without worrying about governmental corruption or health ramifications? There is a better way to consume such items, which I am beginning to figure out for myself.

A simple way for American customers to avoid genetically engineered items is to do what we just did together: carefully read an ingredient list for items like corn syrup and soy lecithin. We live in a very individualized society, where a person can choose whatever he or she wants to eat, from locations all over the world. It seems as if we are in the golden age of food, for how accessible exotic, processed items are. But if someone wants to avoid GMOs, then he or she is best off buying a snack without corn- or soy-derived agents. A good rule is to look for short ingredient lists with names you can pronounce; Pollan suggests trying to eat items with only five ingredients or less as a way to hedge one's bets. Another individual way to respond is to look for organic certification in one's ingredient lists. The recent United States Department of Agriculture organic certification ensures that there are no genetically modified crops used in the food product. Eating healthy has now moved beyond just getting one's vitamins and allotted calories for the day; it is now important to inspect the food for clues that it has been produced in the most natural way possible, without genetic engineering.

While purchasing certain products because of one's ingredient awareness is a successful way to vote with one's dollar, there are greater ways to get involved in trying to shift towards a new direction in this cyclical system. Obviously organic foods are more expensive and less accessible. So it is going to take political participation and grassroots organization to create a new public policy system that makes fresh organic food the more desirable and affordable choice in the supermarket. Organizations have been popping up around the country throughout the last decade or so to petition for clear labeling of genetic modification in processed foods. In Oregon, a concerned mother named Donna Harris created the Oregon Concerned Citizens for Safe Foods that pushed for a referendum to force GMO labeling on local products. While the law got shut down by Monsanto-funded rival campaigns, it still started to spread the word that this food system is not meeting the true health values and needs of its consumers, according to the popular documentary *Food, Inc.* Almost every state has a grassroots organization of some sort, along with large organizations like Greenpeace, that are constantly working towards new policies to change the requirements for these ingredient lists. If a citizen wants to do more than just send a letter to his or her congressional representative about the issue, it is easy to get involved in these campaigns, especially around election times. Citizens have the right to fully utilize their voice in public participation around an issue that is so encompassing and deeply personal.

And even further than that, humans should not accept their position as mindless consumers; for although every person is by nature a consumer, human health and values are beyond simply gobbling up whatever new chemical the FDA approves. Even though our current system allows for processed food to be the cheapest and most accessible, that does not mean it has to be that way in the future. It is vital for citizens to question the policy and technology that is guiding their digestive systems. The average American now has a diet largely dominated by foreign, engineered chemicals, but it has not been this way for very long and does not need to continue this way. I implore citizens to consider what their vision of our future generations will be, what their health will be like, and what their food will look like. Right now, much of our food sounds more like an engineered piece of equipment than a piece of nourishment for one's body. The best way to penetrate a malfunctioning system is to work from within, utilizing the tools of education and policy formation to create a better alternative.

SUGGESTED REFERENCES

www.cornucopia.org
   The Cornucopia Institute, an informative non-profit, investigate organization that provides information on companies to help consumers make educated purchases.

The Omnivore's Dilemma by Michael Pollan
   The first one hundred pages are dedicated to information around genetically engineered corn.

www.responsibletechnology.org
   Institute for Responsible Technology, a research organization outlining major health risks of genetically engineered seed.

HEATHER ROGERS
Sweet & Lowdown

The Ybytymí Hills of eastern Paraguay are crowded with mango trees, palms, and gnarled cacti. Sparse grasses and the red flames of ginger plants dot the ground beneath Brazilian walnut trees, some as tall as 100 feet. It's one of the most biodiverse areas in the world, home to jaguars, tapirs, a plethora of reptiles and amphibians, and more than 500 species of birds.

In a remote area known as Isla Alta, the forest abruptly halts at the edge of sugar fields. The land belongs to a company called Azucarera Paraguaya (AZPA), one of the country's chief sugar producers and the supplier of nearly one-third of the organic sugar consumed in the United States. If you've ever eaten a bowl of Cascadian Farm breakfast cereal or had a glass of Silk soy milk, you've probably enjoyed some of its harvest.

Organic sugar is booming — thanks in part to the spread of organic versions of all the high-sugar snacks Americans love — so much that domestic suppliers can't keep up with demand. Even amid the current recession, organics are the food industry's fastest-growing segment and are still enjoying the double-digit growth rates they've seen over much of the past two decades. Between 2007 and 2008, domestic sales of organics spiked by almost 16 percent to $22.9 billion. But North America has just 7 percent of the world's organic cropland, so organic processors and retailers must increasingly rely on produce from abroad, like raspberries from Chile, asparagus from China, and sugar from Paraguay.

Sugar is a perfect example of how the global organic supply chain works — and why consumers who look for the organic label may not realize what's really behind it. AZPA sells its organic sugar to Wholesome Sweeteners, a subsidiary of Imperial Sugar, America's biggest sugar company. Wholesome in turn sells organic sugar under its own label — as well as to agribusiness giants such as General Mills, which owns the organic brands Cascadian Farm and Muir Glen, and Dean Foods, the maker of Silk. Foreign producers like AZPA that want to sell to the American market must adhere to standards overseen by the US Department of Agriculture's National Organic Program, which have become the de facto organic standards for much of the world. But the enforcement of those rules is spotty, and the rules themselves can be so broad or undefined as to allow practices that seem to violate the spirit of sustainability.

Take clearing old-growth forest to plant new fields — the USDA standards don't even mention it. No one foresaw deforestation as an issue when the National Organic Standards Board began drafting the organic regulations in 1992, according to Fred Kirschenmann, a former board member and sustainable farming expert. However, he says, a land-use rule that would have effectively

118

banned deforestation was rejected. "The National Organic Program's lawyers said no, because devising the metrics for that would be too complex," says Kirschenmann, now a distinguished fellow at the Leopold Center for Sustainable Agriculture at Iowa State University. Asked about this, the NOP says only that organic farming must "maintain or improve" natural resources such as soil and water.

The deforestation loophole gives big growers a cheap way to compete in an aggressive market. "The market needs a certain quantity and quality at a certain price," says Steven Gliessman, a professor of agroecology and environmental studies at the University of California-Santa Cruz. "These are producers that have the resources to buy up unused land, forested areas, and convert them to agricultural land," he says. Organic producers have little incentive not to clear land, says Laura Raynolds, codirector of the Center for Fair and Alternative Trade Studies at Colorado State University. "If they are involved in commercial organic circuits, where price premiums for producers are often quite low, they are caught in the same market dynamics as conventional producers and may disregard rules that are not enforced."

This dynamic was evident when I visited Paraguay, where AZPA has been looking for additional land to grow more organic cane to feed the American market. Converting its conventionally farmed fields to organic would take three years, during which it would have to use more expensive organic methods on "transitional" crops that must be sold at the lower conventional price. A more attractive approach is to establish new fields where forest once grew; then, the cane can fetch the higher organic price from the first harvest.

In Isla Alta I met Flor Fretes, the environmental secretary for the state of Paraguarí, and her husband, Avelino Vega, a local lawmaker and agricultural educator. Both are in their 30s and grew up in the region. Fretes, who had a glamorous mane of black hair and had to change out of short shorts and high heels before we headed into the cane fields, explained that AZPA's land bordered a part of the Ybytymí (pronounced ee-bee-tee-MEE) that's been preserved as a national park. While thousands of acres of AZPA's land were covered with cane, many remained dense with trees. But Vega said that was changing: "Ten years ago there were no roads; it was totally forested." Fretes added, "It's very difficult to fight against. Because AZPA's a big business in the area, everything is just forgotten."

Dario Zaldivar, a Paraguayan who manages US exports for Wholesome Sweeteners, said he'd been trying to convince AZPA to spare the pockets of forest on its undeveloped land at Isla Alta, without much success. He'd noticed more deforested land on AZPA's holdings: "Mostly in the last five years, that's when you can really see it. That's when demand for organic really picked up." Zaldivar wasn't sure if the sugar producer was clearing the land itself. But he speculated that the family-owned company had been shifting its land titles to cattle ranchers, who would clear the land as pasture for two or three years and then sell it back to AZPA. A former militant leftist and founding member of the national Workers' Party, Zaldivar repeatedly told me that the big producers were draining "organic" of its meaning. Asked why he kept working with them, he replied, "Because of the money. In organic you can make a *lot* of money."

When I reached Raúl Hoeckle, then-president of AZPA, at his office in the country's capital, Asunción, he confirmed that his family's company wasn't converting its existing conventional cropland, but was establishing new fields to ramp up organic production. He said AZPA has 25,000 acres in cultivation but would not say how much land it owned altogether. (A Paraguayan government website puts it at 50,000 acres.) When I asked about deforestation, Hoeckle got cross. He said that his family had sold off land only to find, after they'd bought it back, that it had been cleared. "When we sell or buy, our responsibility starts when we buy the land," he explained. "Only then is it important that we don't make something against nature — and we *don't* do it!"

Fretes said it was inconceivable that AZPA could be unaware of the deforestation on what used to be its land. "Even if it's not them doing it directly, even if it's other companies or small farmers, AZPA knows the land is cleared for them to grow sugarcane," she said. "Either way, AZPA is ultimately responsible."

There's nothing illegal about any of this; in fact, it's just one of several opportunities for taking full advantage of the USDA's broad organic standards. On its fields, AZPA follows standards for no-till plowing, weeding by hand, and forgoing chemical fertilizers, herbicides, and insecticides (wasps are used to drive out pests). But AZPA applies chicken manure from industrial poultry farms as fertilizer, a practice that is acceptable under USDA regulations. The regulations ban monocropping, repeatedly growing a single crop in the same field; this applies to annual crops, but not perennials such as sugar. Ruben Ayala, AZPA's head of crop care, told me the company rotates its crops, but he couldn't provide specifics, and I saw no evidence of it. The massive cane fields he showed me had recently been hit by an infestation of sugarcane borers, a common sign of monoculture.

The confusion over what organic really means in practice can be traced back to Washington — specifically, to the offices of the NOP. Since its creation in 2002, the USDA's organic program has suffered from a lack of resources, expertise, and leadership. Until 2008, it subsisted on an annual budget of about $2 million and had between five and eight employees, whose duties included interpreting and enforcing the federal organic rules as well as overseeing nearly 100 certifiers. Just last year, the program's compliance and enforcement branch announced plans to "establish an internal management system" because, for the first time, it was going to have actual staffers.

To be sure, the Obama administration appears to be beefing up the organic program. Recently, its staff nearly doubled from 14 to 27, and its 2010 budget is $7 million. In March, an audit ordered by Kathleen Merrigan, the deputy secretary of agriculture and a longtime proponent of sustainable agriculture,

---

Green on the Outside

What's really behind your organic label?

See No Evil: USDA rules don't require organic produce or the soil it's grown in to be tested for synthetic fertilizers or pesticides.

Substitutions Allowed: The USDA allows 245 nonorganic ingredients in the production of organic foods and livestock. That's up from 77 in 2002. Enjoy the tetrasodium pyrophosphate texturizer in your organic "meat analog product"!

Reality Bites: In 2005, a federal court ruled that organics could not be made with synthetic ingredients. After lobbying by Big Organic, Congress quietly rewrote the law to permit them. More than 50 synthetics are now approved.

Yes You Can: That same revision made it possible to keep using bisphenol A, which has been linked to developmental problems in infants and children, in cans of organic food.

Formula Won: Organic baby formula may contain the synthetic fatty acids DHA and ARA, which may be made using hexane, a potential neurotoxin. USDA staffers who opposed this were overruled after formula makers contacted their boss.

The Grass is Greener: Until February, the USDA only required that organic livestock have "access to pasture." Expanded new rules require meat and dairy cows to graze outside for at least four months a year.

Forest for the Trees: Deforestation isn't prohibited, so growers can chop down old-growth trees to plant organics.

Smells Fishy: The agency is considering organic fish standards that would allow open-net cages that empty waste into the ocean, and nonorganic fish feed that may contain mercury or PCBs.

Skin Deep: The USDA doesn't regulate organic cosmetics or personal care products. While some products do follow the guidelines, many others offer no proof of their claims. Some even count water as an organic ingredient.

Cold Cabbage: The price premium of organic foods over conventional? As much as 350 percent. The penalty for falsely calling your product organic? $10,000.

— Dave Gilson and Heather Rogers

---

concluded that the NOP has failed to consistently oversee organic certifiers or clarify the rules, undermining the "assurance that products labeled as organic are meeting a uniform standard."

Part of the problem is that the enforcement of the organic rules has been left up to third-party certifiers — and the regulations give them plenty of wiggle room. Certifiers are not required to take soil samples or test for chemical residues on produce, only to review paperwork and conduct "visual inspections" — keeping an eye out for containers of banned fertilizers and pesticides. The wide range in how the standards may be interpreted allows producers to shop for a certifier that will apply the rules most favorably.

Until last May, AZPA's certifier was California-based Quality Assurance International, a major player in the global organic trade — it certifies two-thirds of all organic food on US grocery store shelves. Every year, QAI would dispatch a freelance inspector to AZPA's plantation and mill, most recently Luis Brenes, an organic inspector based in Costa Rica. Like QAI, Brenes wouldn't comment on AZPA, but he told me that USDA standards for things such as biodiversity were too vague to include in his inspections, so he had to take the growers' word for it. "If you have a requirement that is not concrete enough to be measured or in some way evaluated, you cannot audit it," he said.

This approach satisfies producers who want organic status and low overhead. But it also opens the door for abuses: In 2007, a USDA investigation found that Aurora Organic Dairy (which supplies Horizon Organics, which is owned by Dean Foods) had committed more than a dozen "willful violations" of organic procedures. QAI, the dairy's certifier, did not revoke its certification, and it continued to defend its client even after the USDA put it on probation. QAI received no penalty. (In its first seven years, the NOP had revoked the licenses of only two organic certifiers.) Joe Smillie, vice president of QAI and a member of the National Organic Standards Board, recently told the *Washington Post*, "People are really hung up on regulations. I say, 'Let's find a way to bend that one, because it's not important.' . . . We live in a polluted world. It isn't pure. We are doing the best we can."

Many consumers continue to give the organic label the benefit of the doubt. Indeed, acknowledges Peter LeCompte, the organic sourcing manager for General Mills, "People's faith in organic is often not founded in knowledge." Is the current certification system susceptible to abuse? "Sure," he says. "If somebody wants to cheat and they're smart, they can get away with it." At an organics industry conference I attended in São Paulo, Brazil, Bruno Fischer, the director of international procurement for the organic conglomerate Hain Celestial, was even more candid. "Most consumers are simple minds," he told the audience. "Simple minds will look at the label and nothing else."

JULIA McLEMORE

You Have One New Notification: Why Facebook Friends Are Not Enough

From ENGS 104, Fall 2010

Last summer, I spent each long, lazy, sweltering day without access to my cell phone or my laptop. To many of my college-aged peers, such a thing is almost unthinkable. And to be honest, it was not by choice. Thanks to two isolated but equally unfortunate accidents (involving a cell phone in a sink and a laptop rolling down the stairs) — as well as a very tight budget for the summer — I was left with no choice but to suffer through three months of being techno-logically disabled. I complained bitterly to my friends (in person, of course) and longed for the days when meeting up for lunch was as easy as a two-second text message. I experienced "phantom vibrations" in my pocket, which would leave me feeling nothing short of ridiculous as I reached towards my jeans to answer a nonexistent phone call. I also lived for the few minutes I'd spend on my Face-book profile when a friend would let me check my email on her computer once every few days. For the first two or three weeks of being "unplugged," it was constantly in the back of my mind that life would be better if I had a cell phone or access to the Internet.

After a little while, however, things surprisingly began to look up. I spent more time doing things I actually enjoyed — like impromptu adventures with friends — now that perusing the Internet for hours on end wasn't an option. Furthermore, I was spending more of my time on and with the people that actually matter to me, instead of fielding texts and status updates from mere acquaintances. Perhaps most surprisingly, I began to notice that I was carrying myself differently in situations that involved me interacting with people I don't know, whether it be making small talk while in line for coffee or having more confidence when applying to jobs. I had figured that without my gadgets, it was only a matter of time before my social life imploded and collapsed. I was wrong. My social life was actually more fulfilling than ever, *and* I finally had some much-needed time to myself. Armed with a new set of social skills that do not include the etiquette of posting on someone's Facebook wall, I began to ques-tion the role that Facebook and other online social networking sites plays in my life and the lives of my peers.

If I were to walk into a random classroom of college students and survey the students about their Internet use, I'd most likely find that virtually every one of them has a Facebook profile. Facebook is a social-networking phenom-enon that has over 500 million active users, more than 50% of which log into their account on any given day. The website has spawned multiple cell phone applications, a best-selling book, and even a critically acclaimed movie starring Justin Timberlake. Facebook originated as an online social network aimed exclusively at college-aged youths like myself, and this age group continues to make up Facebook's most active users. My generation is one slightly obsessed with technology — we are always texting, always tweeting, and always updating our statuses on Facebook. Even the "old-fashioned" phone call is becoming obsolete among my peers.

When my parents were attending college, a friend was a peer you were especially close to and comfortable with. You became friends with someone not through a request, but a rather intimate process of getting to know someone by sharing details of your life with him or her and spending meaningful time together. You had a close group of "best" friends, and a wider circle of acquaintances with whom you connected socially. I, on the other hand, am part of the Facebook generation. In terms of Facebook, a friend is someone whose profile you have full access to; you become friends with someone through a request that requires clicking a button; and you may amass hundreds — maybe thousands — of these "friends." While it would be a stretch to claim that my peers do not know the difference between a friend in "real life" and a Facebook friend, my generation has become increasingly dependent on the latter for social fulfillment — and I'm not the only one who's noticed this. A recent Oxygen Media study found that 57% of the young women they polled communicated with people online more than face-to-face, and young people are logging more hours on the Internet than any age group has ever before. As Facebook friends begin to take up more time in our lives than fellow flesh-and-blood peers, one has to wonder what might be happening socially to my generation. To find out, I began to research what's actually known about the effects of social networking.

10 NEW FRIEND REQUESTS — BUT WHERE ARE YOUR FRIENDS?

While using online social networking sites like Facebook might seem innocent in and of itself, it's the substitution of face-to-face interactions with online socializing that is taking a toll on my generation. In an article for *Psychology Today* entitled "What Facebook Does to Friendships," columnist Jen Kim states, "While the intention behind these sites may be to sustain meaningful relationships, the actual effect has been to help online relationships supplant real life ones." Kim reached this conclusion after interviewing the founder and several members of the website MeetJoe.com, the goal of which is to set up potential pals on "friend dates." Many of the users of this website also spend large amounts of time on social networks such as Facebook. Kim's investigation of the consequences of having primary friendships based on Internet socializing led her to New York University Professor of Psychiatry Irene Levine, who regularly writes for *Psychology Today* on the subject of friendship. Although technology and social media (such as Facebook) have been useful in that they greatly enhance people's ability to communicate instantly across wide distances, they are absolutely not a "substitute for face time," Levine says. According to her, nothing — especially not Facebook — can replace "sitting side-by-side with friends, seeing their facial expressions and body language, and perhaps just saying nothing. There are no quick fixes to making and being friends. It takes quite some time to build trust and connect in an intimate way." Sorry, MeetJoe. com — it's not that easy.

Many of my peers would argue that Facebook is a valuable tool for staying in touch with people we otherwise would not have. While this is not entirely untrue — Facebook can certainly be a useful tool for communicating — I'm skeptical of the generalization of the argument onto ordinary friendships. Being able to see the status updates of the kid who sat behind you in high school calculus is not "staying in touch." And frankly, if you don't care enough or aren't close enough to a person to stay more personally in touch with them, what good does counting them as a Facebook friend do? I know that I personally am a Facebook friend with a large number of people that I would not feel comfortable personally contacting via phone or other method. And yet, I know what these people choose to share with Facebook ("gym/tanning/laundry text meeee!"). It seems a little backwards . . . and it is.

In an article addressing what he calls the "technology-intimacy tradeoff," *Psychology Today* columnist David Lundberg Kenrick says, "Relationships with families, lovers, and friends, are costly. Modern technology — in the form of planes that allow us to move far away, and communication devices such as cell phones and computers that allow us to maintain some semblance of contact — can free us from those costs." Research on the subject, however, has found that this "freedom" comes at an enormous price. At Carnegie Mellon University, researcher Robert Kraut and colleagues used longitudinal data from 73 households over two years to look at the social effects of using the Internet for communication. The results of the study suggest that while the Internet is indeed a useful tool for communication, the more a household member's Internet use increased, the more his or her communication with other members of the house decreased, the smaller his or her social circle became, and instances of depression and loneliness increased.

Ersatz social engagement theory proposes that individuals may be drawn to communicating via methods such as Facebook or text messaging because they are easier, less risky, and more immediately gratifying than face-to-face interactions. However, despite this initial trade-off, researcher Melanie Green and colleagues proposed that such interactions would prove to be less satisfying over the long term. In their study, they tested the moods of 42 participants before and after engaging with a stranger either face-to-face or online via instant messaging. The results showed that the people communicating online were happier immediately after the interaction than those who communicated face-to-face;

however, when Green followed up with participants and surveyed them on their Internet use, those who used instant messaging more often reported reduced life satisfaction. Generally, research has found that the more a person's ratio of online social engagements to real life conversations increases, the more his or her general life satisfaction decreases. In short, Facebook friends are not enough — not even close.

THE FACEBOOK EVOLUTION

The next edition of the Diagnostic and Statistical Manual of Mental Disorders (DSM) will most likely include something called "Internet Addiction Disorder," describing those who suffer from it as people who have become so dependent on extensive Internet use that it hugely impedes their daily functioning. A possible subset of this disorder may very well be Facebook Addiction Disorder, accounting for most cases of IAD among college-aged persons. But increasing Facebook and Internet use is doing more than just making us unhappy. It's also changing the way my generation navigates our social lives, from how we interact with potential romantic partners to how we deal with situations involving total strangers.

The fact of the matter is, many of my peers are comfortable connecting on a superficial level with hundreds of people on Facebook, but the idea of introducing one's self and starting a conversation with a stranger is hugely daunting. Similarly, I know from personal experience that unless the person I'm contacting is someone I'm very close to, I'll always prefer to send someone a text than to call her and engage in an actual, real-time conversation. While I'm in no way arguing that mine is a generation of socially inept gadget addicts — personally, I think of myself as relatively friendly and outgoing — I believe that it's true that my peers and I have been so busy texting and checking our Facebook profiles that we really do lack some of the face-to-face social skills that generations before us had no choice but to develop.

John Elder, a writer for *Psychology Today* and an individual living with high-functioning autism, suggests that the Facebook generation's increasing replacement of face-to-face interactions with social networking use is creating a social culture that mirrors Asperger's syndrome. My peers and I are losing the social skills needed to pick up on nonverbal cues, body language, and facial expressions because of a kind of "computer enhanced evolution" — says Elder, "Our brains build up the neural pathways we use, and prune the ones we ignore. Yesterday's paths led us to your friend next door, and the girl in Social Studies and maybe Uncle Bob. Tomorrow's paths lead through the Xbox to some game enthusiast in China, and through the Blackberry to a likeminded person in Canada." When my mother was in college, Blackberry messaging and Facebook chatting were not options when she wanted or needed to get in contact with someone. If she was shy or uncomfortable calling someone or (heaven forbid) knocking on someone's door, she simply had to get over it. My generation does not. Instead, we hide behind our technology.

Elder quotes in his article, "Many of today's young people learn the subtleties of text messaging and email. They say, I can be connected to the whole world electronically, and that's true in a sense. The problem is, that electronic connectedness may come at the expense of learning how to act on a date, or in a group, or at a party. And those are vital skills that every young person needs."

These "vital skills" can only be acquired one way: experiencing and engaging in face-to-face, real life social interactions . . . and often.

UNPLUGGED: LESSONS FROM A LOW-TECH SUMMER

As I explained at the beginning of this article, I spent the majority of the summer without a cell phone or a laptop. It was an immensely enlightening experience, and I've come away with it having a new appreciation of turning off my cell phone and logging out of Facebook. My generation doesn't have to get personal, so we're generally not good at it. And I think we're missing out. We can read and edit all of our texts infinite times before we send them, protecting ourselves form saying something in the moment that might make us vulnerable. We can use our computers and our phones to initiate plans with friends, protecting ourselves from the possible rejection that is sometimes unavoidable when a conversation with someone is more than a Facebook message thread. And we can establish romantic relationships via an option on our Facebook profiles and text our carefully edited feelings to someone we care about (and want to have care about us), instead of trying to ignore that queasy nervous feeling in the pit of our stomachs as we look somebody in the eyes and struggle to find the words that express what we need to say. For a generation of social networking butterflies, we are always so cautious, sometimes even afraid.

This summer, I did often miss my cell phone, laptop, and the Internet — and I think that's okay. Social networking is popular because a lot of the time, it's fun. But as the summer progressed, I found myself truly relaxing in a way I don't usually experience. I was finally unplugged. And it wasn't that I was some kind of Walden Pond-esque recluse, but that without the background noise of status updates, friend requests, and picture comments, I found myself primarily connecting with the people who are truly important to me, the people whose doors I do feel comfortable knocking on. It's these kinds of interactions that are truly fulfilling, and that truly increase your satisfaction in life. While Facebook friends are no doubt fun, it's the face-to-face social engagements you experience that add richness to the texture of life.

I'm not arguing for a mass exodus from Facebook or Blackberrys among my friends; instead, I'm urging my age group to unplug themselves every so often and to occasionally take small risks that put themselves out there on a more personal level. Because constantly hiding behind your cell phone keyboard or computer screen protects you, yes, but it also causes you to miss out on the rewarding experience of making face-to-face connections. So silence your cell phone when you're on a date (even better, leave it at home); call your friends to make plans, don't text them; and most importantly, when you have something to say that makes you nervous — like, "I love you" — say it in person. It's always worth the risk.

PROJECT 5

Narrowing/Expanding the Focus

DAVID FOSTER WALLACE
Forever Overhead
From *Brief Interviews with Hideous Men*

Happy Birthday. Your thirteenth is important. Maybe your first really public day. Your thirteenth is the chance for people to recognize that important things are happening to you.

Things have been happening to you for the past half year. You have seven hairs in your left armpit now. Twelve in your right. Hard dangerous spirals of brittle black hair. Crunchy, animal hair. There are now more of the hard curled hairs around your privates than you can count without losing track. Other things. Your voice is rich and scratchy and moves between octaves without any warning. Your face has begun to get shiny when you don't wash it. And two weeks of a deep and frightening ache this past spring left you with something dropped down from inside: your sack is now full and vulnerable, a commodity to be protected. Hefted and strapped in tight supporters that stripe your buttocks red. You have grown into a new fragility.

And dreams. For months there have been dreams like nothing before: moist and busy and distant, full of yielding curves, frantic pistons, warmth and a great falling; and you have awakened through fluttering lids to a rush and a gush and a toe-curling scalp-snapping jolt of feeling from an inside deeper than you knew you had, spasms of a deep sweet hurt, the streetlights through your window blinds cracking into sharp stars against the black bedroom ceiling, and on you a dense white jam that lisps between legs, trickles and sticks, cools on you, hardens and clears until there is nothing but gnarled knots of pale solid animal hair in the morning shower, and in the wet tangle a clean sweet smell you can't believe comes from anything you made inside you.

The smell is, more than anything, like this swimming pool: a bleached sweet salt, a flower with chemical petals. The pool has a strong clear blue smell, though you know the smell is never as strong when you are actually in the blue water, as you are now, all swum out, resting back along the shallow end, the hip-high water lapping at where it's all changed.

Around the deck of this old public pool on the western edge of Tucson is a Cyclone fence the color of pewter, decorated with a bright tangle of locked bicycles. Beyond this a hot black parking lot full of white lines and glittering cars. A dull field of dry grass and hard weeds, old dandelions' downy heads exploding and snowing up in a rising wind. And past all this, reddened by a round slow September sun, are mountains, jagged, their tops' sharp angles darkening into definition against a deep red tired light. Against the red their sharp connected tops form a spiked line, an EKG of the dying day.

The clouds are taking on color by the rim of the sky. The water is spangles off soft blue, five-o'clock warm, and the pool's smell, like the other smell, connects with a chemical haze inside you, an interior dimness that bends light to its own ends, softens the difference between what leaves off and what begins.

Your party is tonight. This afternoon, on your birthday, you have asked to come to the pool. You wanted to come alone, but a birthday is a family day, your family wants to be with you. This is nice, and you can't talk about why you wanted to come alone, and really truly maybe you didn't want to come alone, so they are here. Sunning. Both your parents sun. Their deck chairs have been marking time all afternoon, rotating, tracking the sun's curve across a desert sky heated to an eggy film. Your sister plays Marco Polo near you in the shallows with a group of thin girls from her grade. She is being blind now, her Marco's being Polo'd. She is shut-eyed and twirling to different cries, spinning at the hub of a wheel of shrill girls in bathing caps. Her cap has raised rubber flowers. There are limp old pink petals that shake as she lunges at blind sound.

There at the other end of the pool is the diving tank and the high board's tower. Back on the deck behind is the SN CK BAR, and on either side, bolted above the cement entrances to dark wet showers and lockers, are gray metal bullhorn speakers that send out the pool's radio music, the jangle flat and tinny thin.

Your family likes you. You are bright and quiet, respectful to elders — though you are not without spine. You are largely good. You look out for your little sister. You are her ally. You were six when she was zero and you had the mumps when they brought her home in a very soft yellow blanket; you kissed her hello on her feet out of concern that she not catch your mumps. Your parents say that this augured well. That it set the tone. They now feel they were right. In all things they are proud of you, satisfied, and they have retreated to the warm distance from which pride and satisfaction travel. You all get along well.

Happy Birthday. It is a big day, big as the roof of the whole southwest sky. You have thought it over. There is the high board. They will want to leave soon. Climb out and do the thing.

Shake off the blue clean. You're half-bleached, loose and soft, tenderized, pads of fingers wrinkled. The mist of the pool's too clean smell is in your eyes; it breaks light into gentle color. Knock your head with the heel of your hand. One side has a flabby echo. Cock your head to the side and hop — sudden heat in your ear, delicious, and brain-warmed water turns cold on the nautilus of your ear's outside. You can hear harder tinnier music, closer shouts, much movement in much water.

The pool is crowded for this late. Here are thin children, hairy animal men. Disproportionate boys, all necks and legs and knobby joints, shallowchested, vaguely birdlike. Like you. Here are old people moving tentatively through shallows on stick legs, feeling at the water with their hands, out of every element at once.

And girl-women, women, curved like instruments or fruit, skin burnished brown-bright, suit tops held by delicate knots of fragile colored string against the pull of mysterious weights, suit bottoms riding low over the gentle juts of hips totally unlike your own, immoderate swells and swivels that melt in light into a surrounding space that cups and accommodates the soft curves as things precious. You almost understand.

The pool is a system of movement. Here now there are: laps, splash fights, dives, corner tag, cannonballs, Sharks and Minnows, high fallings, Marco Polo (your sister still It, halfway to tears, too long to be It, the game teetering on the edge of cruelty, not your business to save or embarrass). Two clean little bright-white boys caped in cotton towels run along the poolside until the guard stops them dead with a shout through his bullhorn. The guard is brown as a tree, blond hair in a vertical line on his stomach, his head in a jungle explorer hat, his nose a white triangle of cream. A girl has an arm around a leg of his little tower. He's bored.

Get out now and go past your parents, who are sunning and reading, not looking up. Forget your towel. Stopping for the towel means talking and talking means thinking. You have decided being scared is caused mostly by thinking. Go right by, toward the tank at the deep end. Over the tank is a great iron tower of dirty white. A board protrudes from the top of the tower like a tongue. The pool's concrete deck is rough and hot against your bleached feet. Each of your footprints is thinner and fainter. Each shrinks behind you on the hot stone and disappears.

Lines of plastic wieners bob around the tank, which is entirely its own thing, empty of the rest of the pool's convulsive ballet of heads and arms. The tank is blue as energy, small and deep and perfectly square, flanked by lap lanes and SN CK BAR and rough hot deck and the bent late shadow of the tower and board. The tank is quiet and still and healed smooth between fallings.

There is a rhythm to it. Like breathing. Like a machine. The line for the board curves back from the tower's ladder. The line moves in its curve, straightens as it nears the ladder. One by one, people reach the ladder and climb. One by one, spaced by the beat of hearts, they reach the tongue of the board at the top. And once on the board, they pause, each exactly the same tiny heart-beat pause. And their legs take them to the end, where they all give the same sort of stomping hop, arms curving out as if to describe something circular, total; they come down heavy on the edge of the board and make it throw them up and out.

It's a swooping machine, lines of stuttered movement in a sweet late bleach mist. You can watch from the deck as they hit the cold blue sheet of the tank. Each fall makes a white that plumes and falls into itself and spreads and fizzes. Then blue clean comes up in the middle of the white and spreads like pudding, making it all new. The tank heals itself. Three times as you go by.

You are in line. Look around. Look bored. Few talk in the line. Everyone seems by himself. Most look at the ladder, look bored. You almost all have crossed arms, chilled by a late dry rising wind on the constellations of blue-clean chlorine beads that cover your backs and shoulders. It seems impossible that everybody could really be this bored. Beside you is the edge of the tower's shadow, the tilted black tongue of the board's image. The system of shadow is huge, long, off to the side, joined to the tower's base at a sharp late angle.

Almost everyone in line for the board watches the ladder. Older boys watch older girls' bottoms as they go up. The bottoms are in soft thin cloth, tight nylon stretch. The good bottoms move up the ladder like pendulums in liquid, a gentle uncrackable code. The girls' legs make you think of deer. Look bored.

Look out past it. Look across. You can see so well. Your mother is in her deck chair, reading, squinting, her face tilted up to get light on her cheeks. She hasn't looked to see where you are. She sips something sweet out of a bright can. Your father is on his big stomach, back like the hint of a hump of a whale, shoulders curling with animal spirals, skin oiled and soaked red-brown with too much sun. Your towel is hanging off your chair and a corner of the cloth now moves — your mother hit it as she waved away a sweat bee that likes what she has in the can. The bee is back right away, seeming to hang motionless over the can in a sweet blur. Your towel is one big face of Yogi Bear.

At some point there has gotten to be more line behind you than in front of you. Now no one in front except three on the slender ladder. The woman right before you is on the low rungs, looking up, wearing a tight black nylon suit that is all one piece. She climbs. From above there is a rumble, then a great falling, then a plume and the tank reheals. Now two on the ladder. The pool rules say one on the ladder at a time, but the guard never shouts about it. The guard makes the real rules by shouting or not shouting.

This woman above you should not wear a suit as tight as the suit she is wearing. She is as old as your mother, and as big. She is too big and too white. Her suit is full of her. The backs of her thighs are squeezed by the suit and look like cheese. Her legs have abrupt little squiggles of cold blue shattered vein under the white skin, as if something were broken, hurt, in her legs. Her legs look like they hurt to be squeezed, full of curled Arabic lines of cold broken blue. Her legs make you feel like your own legs hurt.

The rungs are very thin. It's unexpected. Thin round iron rungs laced in slick wet Safe-T felt. You taste metal from the smell of wet iron in shadow. Each rung presses into the bottoms of your feet and dents them. The dents feel deep and they hurt. You feel heavy. How the big woman over you must feel. The handrails along the ladder's sides are also very thin. It's like you might not hold on. You've got to hope the woman holds on, too. And of course it looked like fewer rungs from far away. You are not stupid.

Get halfway up, up in the open, big woman placed above you, a solid bald muscular man on the ladder underneath your feet. The board is still high overhead, invisible from here. But it rumbles and makes a heavy flapping sound, and a boy you can see for a few contained feet through the thin rungs falls in a flash of a line, a knee held to his chest, doing a splasher. There is a huge exclamation point of foam up into your field of sight, then scattered claps into a great fizzing. Then the silent sound of the tank healing to new blue all over again.

More thin rungs. Hold on tight. The radio is loudest here, one speaker at ear-level over a concrete locker room entrance. A cool dank whiff of the locker room inside. Grab the iron bars tight and twist and look down behind you and you can see people buying snacks and refreshments below. You can see down into it: the clean white top of the vendor's cap, rubs of ice cream, steaming brass freezers, scuba tanks of soft drink syrup, snakes of soda hose, bulging boxes of salty popcorn kept hot in the sun. Now that you're overhead you can see the whole thing.

There's wind. It's windier the higher you get. The wind is thin; through the shadow it's cold on your wet skin. On the ladder in the shadow your skin looks very white. The wind makes a thin whistle in your ears. Four more rungs to the top of the tower. The rungs hurt your feet. They are thin and let you know just how much you weigh. You have real weight on the ladder. The ground wants you back.

Now you can see just over the top of the ladder. You can see the board. The woman is there. There are two ridges of red, hurt-looking callus on the backs of her ankles. She stands at the start of the board, your eyes on her ankles. Now you're up above the tower's shadow. The solid man under you is looking through the rungs into the contained space the woman's fall will pass through.

She pauses for just that beat of a pause. There's nothing slow about it at all. It makes you cold. In no time she's at the end of the board, up, down on it, it bends low like it doesn't want her. Then it nods and flaps and throws her violently up and out, her arms opening out to inscribe that circle, and gone. She disappears in a dark blink. And there's time before you hear the hit below.

Listen. It does not seem good, the way she disappears into a time that passes before she sounds. Like a stone down a well. But you think she did not think so. She was part of a rhythm chat excludes thinking. And now you have made yourself part of it, too. The rhythm seems blind. Like ants. Like a machine.

You decide this needs to be thought about. It may, after all, be all right to do something scary without thinking, but not when the scariness is the not thinking itself. Not when not thinking turns out to be wrong. At some point the wrongnesses have piled up blind: pretend-boredom, weight, thin rungs, hurt feet, space cut into laddered parts that melt together only in a disappearance that takes time. The wind on the ladder not what anyone would have expected. The way the board protrudes from shadow into light and you can't see past the end. When it all turns out to be different you should get to think. It should be required.

The ladder is full beneath you. Stacked up, everyone a few rungs apart. The ladder is fed by a solid line that stretches back and curves into the dark of the tower's canted shadow. People's arms are crossed in the line. Those on the ladder's feet hurt and they are all looking up. It is a machine that moves only forward.

Climb up onto the tower's tongue. The board turns out to be long. As long as the time you stand there. Time slows. It thickens around you as your heart gets more and more beats out of every second, every movement in the system of the pool below.

The board is long. From where you stand it seems to stretch off into nothing. It's going to send you someplace which its own length keeps you from seeing, which seems wrong to submit to without even thinking.

Looked at another way, the same board is just a long thin flat thing covered with a rough white plastic stuff. The white surface is very rough and is freckled and lined with a pale watered red that is nevertheless still red and not yet pink — drops of old pool water that are catching the light of the late sun over sharp mountains. The rough white stuff of the board is wet. And cold. Your feet are hurt from the thin rungs and have a great ability to feel. They feel your weight. There are handrails running above the beginning of the board. They are not like the ladder's handrails just were. They are thick and set very low, so you almost have to bend over to hold on to them. They are just for show, no one holds them. Holding on takes time and alters the rhythm of the machine.

It is a long cold rough white plastic or fiberglass board, veined with the sad near-pink color of bad candy.

But at the end of the white board, the edge, where you'll come down with your weight to make it send you off, there are two areas of darkness. Two flat shadows in the broad light. Two vague black ovals. The end of the board has two dirty spots.

They are from all the people who've gone before you. Your feet as you stand here are tender and dented, hurt by the rough wet surface, and you see that the two dark spots are from people's skin. They are skin abraded from feet by the violence of the disappearance of people with real weight. More people than you could count without losing track. The weight and abrasion of their disappearance leaves little bits of soft tender feet behind, bits and shards and curls of skin that dirty and darken and tan as they lie tiny and smeared in the sun at the end of the board. They pile up and get smeared and mixed together. They darken in two circles.

No time is passing outside you at all. It is amazing. The late ballet below is slow motion, the overbroad movements of mimes in blue jelly. If you wanted you could really stay here forever, vibrating inside so fast you float motionless in time, like a bee over something sweet.

But they should clean the board. Anybody who thought about it for even a second would see that they should clean the end of the board of people's skin, of two black collections of what's left of before, spots that from back here look like eyes, like blind and cross-eyed eyes.

Where you are now is still and quiet. Wind radio shouting splashing not here. No time and no real sound but your blood squeaking in your head.

Overhead here means sight and smell. The smells are intimate, newly clear. The smell of bleach's special flower, but out of it other things rise to you like a weed's seeded snow. You smell deep yellow popcorn. Sweet tan oil like hot coconut. Either hot dogs or corn dogs. A thin cruel hint of very dark Pepsi in paper cups. And the special smell of tons of water coming off tons of skin, rising like steam off a new bath. Animal heat. From overhead it is more real than anything.

Look at it. You can see the whole complicated thing, blue and white and brown and white, soaked in a watery spangle of deepening red. Everybody. This is what people call a view. And you knew that from below you wouldn't look nearly so high overhead. You see now how high overhead you are. You knew from down there no one could tell.

He says it behind you, his eyes on your ankles, the solid bald man, Hey kid. They want to know. Do your plans up here involve the whole day or what exactly is the story. Hey kid are you okay.

There's been time this whole time. You can't kill time with your heart. Everything takes time. Bees have to move very fast to stay still.

Hey kid he says Hey kid are you okay.

Metal flowers bloom on your tongue. No more time for thinking. Now that there is time you don't have time.

Hey.

Slowly now, out across everything, there's a watching that spreads like hit water's rings. Watch it spread out from the ladder. Your sighted sister and her thin white pack, pointing. Your mother looks to the shallows where you used to be, then makes a visor of her hand. The whale stirs and jiggles. The guard looks up, the girl around his leg looks up, he reaches for his horn.

Forever below is rough deck, snacks, thin metal music, down where you once used to be; the line is solid and has no reverse gear; and the water, of course, is only soft when you're inside it. Look down. Now it moves in the sun, full of hard coins of light that shimmer red as they stretch away into a mist that is your own sweet salt. The coins crack into new moons, long shards of light from the hearts of sad stars. The square tank is a cold blue sheet. Cold is just a kind of hard. A kind of blind. You have been taken off guard. Happy Birthday. Did you think it over. Yes and no. Hey kid.

Two black spots, violence, and disappear into a well of time. Height is not the problem. It all changes when you get back down. When you hit, with your weight.

So which is the lie? Hard or soft? Silence or time?

The lie is that it's one or the other. A still, floating bee is moving faster than it can think. From overhead the sweetness drives it crazy.

The board will nod and you will go, and eyes of skin can cross blind into a cloud-blotched sky, punctured light emptying behind sharp stone that is forever. That is forever. Step into the skin and disappear.

Hello.

SARA STANTON
Sticks and Stones
Revised

As an openly gay woman, each time I hear a homophobic slur, the words stick with me. Regardless of who uses words like faggot or dyke, and in what context, each utterance brings me back to the days when my sexuality was a consuming, daunting secret. Whether used in unintentional or deliberate homophobia, or out of ignorance, the single constant is that someone is victimized with each homophobic remark. The intentions of the person speaking these words cannot and do not qualify the effect; it does not hurt any less when someone does not *intend* to inflict pain.

When I was 14 and only in 8th grade, I decided to apply to boarding school. While many factors ultimately contributed to my decision to attend boarding school, the primary reason was one of hope. I knew that there was something different about me, and I hoped boarding school would give me the freedom to discover why I felt different. I was accepted to one of the most prestigious prep schools in the country, and at first I felt lucky — even invincible. It didn't take long for me to understand that I was different because I was gay; however, I learned this the hard way. I had only been on campus for a few hours before I started hearing "That's so gay" and "faggot" in almost every conversation. The words seemed to sink into me while others had no trouble not only continuing their days unaffected by the words, but also utilizing them. These words were inculcated into my head for weeks until finally I spoke up.

"Don't use that word," I told a girl on my soccer team.

"Why not? What are you, a dyke?" she snapped.

Although rhetorical, her inquiry forced me to look in the mirror. I replayed the moment over and over in my head and, for the first time, understood that I was, in fact, undeniably gay. However, the homophobia at my high school was so pervasive, so destructive, that I suppressed my secret until my junior year, when it spilled out of me like blood. I only told my closest friends, but it didn't take long before students I had never spoken to were shoving me into walls and whispering, "Stay away from my girlfriend, faggot." Ultimately, harassment and bullying because of my sexuality defined my high school experience. It was tormenting and traumatic, and the majority of students were deliberately and admittedly homophobic. Their constant use of homophobic slurs suffocated my secret. Their words forced me to hold my own back, thereby preventing me from being myself.

Even the unintentional slips by my peers were disparaging. Their homophobic language did not exist in a vacuum. It was not simply a jab at a friend;

139

it was a constant reminder that there was something wrong with being gay — something wrong with me. The language created a hostile, unsafe environment, and perpetuated an enduring stereotype that being gay makes you weak or less human.

Surviving homophobic speech in high school became a full-time, every-day job, one that made me so physically ill that I was diagnosed with depression in my senior year. One of my friends once asked me why the words got to me so much. "Sticks and stones," she said. To someone who is not sensitive to ho-mophobia, it may seem as though each use of homophobic language is isolated and unrelated to the next. To me, however, each utterance built upon the pre-vious. Each one was a bullet, some from unsuspecting friends and others from strangers, creating a constant feeling of having to be on the defense.

My experiences in high school contributed to my decision to come to UVM. Before I visited, I had heard about the liberal, welcoming community in Burlington. I heard that UVM was a place where one's sexuality was not as-sumed or judged, it was one puzzle piece out of thousands that create an indi-vidual. Of course, homophobia exists even in the most liberal of places, but I have witnessed it in a much different way here.

In my first weeks at UVM, I did not hide my sexuality. It was, in many ways, a dream for me. Then, one day, in a friend's dorm room, I heard him say, "Dude, this assignment is so gay." I looked up, puzzled. He immediately turned to me. "Gay doesn't mean homosexual anymore. Just like it changed from meaning happy, now it means stupid — it doesn't have anything to do with gay people anymore."

I truly believe that he did not intend to hurt me or in any way offend the gay community. However, he did bring me back to my days in high school when I felt helpless and voiceless. What's more, if someone who did not know him had overheard his comment, they may have had a vastly different image of him. Out of context, he may have been indistinguishable between an open-minded UVM student, and a homophobic student from my high school, simply because of his word choice. In that regard, ignorance is not an excuse and does not dull the pain for someone who is the target of homophobic speech.

In Vermont, I am a much different person than I was in high school. Here, I feel safe and confident enough to speak up, and that is an invaluable comfort. However, homophobic slurs are far too commonplace to truly represent the ideals of our school. I constantly hear boys calling each other faggots, and often in my presence they will clarify that they are not directly speaking about *me*, they are calling their friends weak or feminine. This, like my friend's use of the word "gay," is no less hurtful than intentional, deliberate homophobia. The word "faggot" is an unarguably pejorative term referring to homosexuals. Used on campus, it often does delineate a sense of weakness or a lack of manhood. Faggot is an offensive word and encompasses all gay people. One cannot simply say that their use of the word faggot only applies to certain people, just as one cannot say the word nigger does not apply to all black people.

Language is one of many factors contributing to the continuation of homophobia. To use derogatory language, even in jest, is to give permission to hateful, homophobic people everywhere to use those words themselves by making the words colloquial. When words become colloquial, they lose their shock value, and we stop questioning what they really mean and how much they can hurt. Although many people argue America is becoming a more gay-friendly country both legally and socially, there were as many as 6 suicides in September of this year as a direct result of homophobia in schools. This statistic is an alarming indication that everyone, no matter what their sexuality, must be more aware of the words they choose and the people they may hurt, regardless of intention.

PATRICIA WILLIAMS

The Death of the Profane
(a commentary on the genre
of legal writing)

From *The Alchemy of Race and Rights*

Buzzers are big in New York City. Favored particularly by smaller stores and boutiques, merchants throughout the city have installed them as screening devices to reduce the incidence of robbery: if the face at the door looks desirable, the buzzer is pressed and the door is unlocked. If the face is that of an undesirable, the door stays locked. Predictably, the issue of undesirability has revealed itself to be a racial determination. While controversial enough at first, even civil-rights organizations backed down eventually in the face of arguments that the buzzer system is a "necessary evil," that it is a "mere inconvenience" in comparison to the risks of being murdered, that suffering discrimination is not as bad as being assaulted, and that in any event it is not all blacks who are barred, just "17-year-old black males wearing running shoes and hooded sweatshirts."[1]

The installation of these buzzers happened swiftly in New York; stores that had always had their doors wide open suddenly became exclusive or received people by appointment only. I discovered them and their meaning one Saturday in 1986. I was shopping in Soho and saw in a store window a sweater that I wanted to buy for my mother. I pressed my round brown face to the window and my finger to the buzzer, seeking admittance. A narrow-eyed, white teenager wearing running shoes and feasting on bubble gum glared out, evaluating me for signs that would pit me against the limits of his social understanding. After about five seconds, he mouthed "We're closed," and blew pink rubber at me. It was two Saturdays before Christmas, at one o'clock in the afternoon; there were several white people in the store who appeared to be shopping for things for *their* mothers.

I was enraged. At that moment I literally wanted to break all the windows of the store and *take* lots of sweaters for my mother. In the flicker of his judgmental gray eyes, that saleschild had transformed my brightly sentimental, joy-to-the-world, pre-Christmas spree to a shambles. He snuffed my sense of humanitarian catholicity, and there was nothing I could do to snuff his, without making a spectacle of myself.

I am still struck by the structure of power that drove me into such a blizzard of rage. There was almost nothing I could do, short of physically intruding upon him, that would humiliate him the way he humiliated me. No words, no

142

gestures, no prejudices of my own would make a bit of difference to him; his refusal to let me into the store — it was Benetton's, whose colorfully punnish ad campaign is premised on wrapping every one of the world's peoples in its cottons and woolens — was an outward manifestation of his never having let someone like me into the realm of his reality. He had no compassion, no remorse, no reference to me; and no desire to acknowledge me even at the estranged level of arm's-length transactor. He saw me only as one who would take his money and therefore could not conceive that I was there to give him money.

In this weird ontological imbalance, I realized that buying something in that store was like bestowing a gift, the gift of my commerce, the lucre of my patronage. In the wake of my outrage, I wanted to take back the gift of appreciation that my peering in the window must have appeared to be. I wanted to take it back in the form of unappreciation, disrespect, defilement. I wanted to work so hard at wishing he could feel what I felt that he would never again mistake my hatred for some sort of plaintive wish to be included. I was quite willing to disenfranchise myself, in the heat of my need to revoke the flattery of my purchasing power. I was willing to boycott Benetton's, random white-owned businesses, and anyone who ever blew bubble gum in my face again.

My rage was admittedly diffuse, even self-destructive, but it was symmetrical. The perhaps loose-ended but utter propriety of that rage is no doubt lost not just to the young man who actually barred me, but to those who would appreciate my being barred only as an abstract precaution, who approve of those who would bar even as they deny that they would bar *me*.

The violence of my desire to burst into Benetton's is probably quite apparent. I often wonder if the violence, the exclusionary hatred, is equally apparent in the repeated public urgings that blacks understand the buzzer system by putting themselves in the shoes of white storeowners — that, in effect, blacks look into the mirror of frightened white faces for the reality of their undesirability; and that then blacks would "just as surely conclude that [they] would not let [themselves] in under similar circumstances."[2] (That some blacks might agree merely shows that some of us have learned too well the lessons of privatized intimacies of self-hatred and rationalized away the fullness of our public, participatory selves.)

On the same day I was barred from Benetton's, I went home and wrote the above impassioned account in my journal. On the day after that, I found I was still brooding, so I turned to a form of catharsis I have always found healing. I typed up as much of the story as I have just told, made a big poster of it, put a nice colorful border around it, and, after Benetton's was truly closed, stuck it to their big sweater-filled window. I exercised my first-amendment right to place my business with them right out in the street.

So that was the first telling of this story. The second telling came a few months later, for a symposium on Excluded Voices sponsored by a law review. I wrote an essay summing up my feelings about being excluded from Benetton's and analyzing "how the rhetoric of increased privatization, in response to racial issues, functions as the rationalizing agent of public unaccountability and, ultimately, irresponsibility." Weeks later, I received the first edit. From the first page to the last, my fury had been carefully cut out. My rushing, run-on-rage had been reduced to simple declarative sentences. The active personal had been inverted in favor of the passive impersonal. My words were different; they spoke to me upsidedown. I was afraid to read too much of it at a time — meanings rose up at me oddly, stolen and strange.

A week and a half later, I received the second edit. All reference to Benetton's had been deleted because, according to the editors and the faculty adviser, it was defamatory; they feared harassment and liability; they said printing it would be irresponsible. I called them and offered to supply a footnote attesting to this as my personal experience at one particular location and of a buzzer system not limited to Benetton's; the editors told me that they were not in the habit of publishing things that were unverifiable. I could not but wonder, in this refusal even to let me file an affidavit, what it would take to make my experience verifiable. The testimony of an independent white bystander? (a requirement in fact imposed in U.S. Supreme Court holdings through the first part of the century[3]).

Two days *after* the piece was sent to press, I received copies of the final page proofs. All reference to my race had been eliminated because it was against "editorial policy" to permit descriptions of physiognomy. "I realize," wrote one editor, "that this was a very personal experience, but any reader will know what you must have looked like when standing at that window." In a telephone conversation to them, I ranted wildly about the significance of such an omission. "It's irrelevant," another editor explained in a voice gummy with soothing and patience; "It's nice and poetic," but it doesn't "advance the discussion of any principle . . . This is a law review, after all." Frustrated, I accused him of censorship; calmly he assured me it was not. "This is just a matter of style," he said with firmness and finality.

Ultimately I did convince the editors that mention of my race was central to the whole sense of the subsequent text; that my story became one of extreme paranoia without the information that I am black; or that it became one in which the reader had to fill in the gap by assumption, presumption, prejudgment, or prejudice. What was most interesting to me in this experience was how the blind application of principles of neutrality, through the device of omission, acted either to make me look crazy or to make the reader participate in old habits of cultural bias.

That was the second telling of my story. The third telling came last April, when I was invited to participate in a law-school conference on Equality and Difference. I retold my sad tale of exclusion from Soho's most glitzy boutique, focusing in this version on the law-review editing process as a consequence of an ideology of style rooted in a social text of neutrality. I opined:

Law and legal writing aspire to formalized, color-blind, liberal ideals. Neutrality is the standard for assuring these ideals; yet the adherence to it is often determined by reference to an aesthetic of uniformity, in which difference is simply omitted. For example, when segregation was eradicated from the American lexicon, its omission led many to actually believe that racism therefore no longer existed. Race-neutrality in law has become the presumed antidote for race bias in real life. With the entrenchment of the notion of race-neutrality came attacks on the concept of affirmative action and the rise of reverse discrimination suits. Blacks, for so many generations deprived of jobs based on the color of our skin, are now told that we ought to find it demeaning to be hired, based on the color of our skin. Such is the silliness of simplistic either-or inversions as remedies to complex problems.

What is truly demeaning in this era of double-speak-no-evil is going on interviews and not getting hired because someone doesn't think we'll be comfortable. It is demeaning not to get promoted because we're judged "too weak," then putting in a lot of energy the next time and getting fired because we're "too strong." It is demeaning to be told what we find demeaning. It is very demeaning to stand on street corners unemployed and begging. It is downright demeaning to have to explain why we haven't been employed for months and then watch the job go to someone who is "more experienced." It is outrageously demeaning that none of this can be called racism, even if it happens only to, or to large numbers of, black people; as long as it's done with a smile, a handshake and a shrug; as long as the phantom-word "race" is never used.

The image of race as a phantom-word came to me after I moved into my late godmother's home. In an attempt to make it my own, I cleared the bedroom for painting. The following morning the room asserted itself, came rushing and raging at me through the emptiness, exactly as it had been for twenty-five years. One day filled with profuse and overwhelming complexity, the next day filled with persistently recurring memories. The shape of the past came to haunt me, the shape of the emptiness confronted me each time I was about to enter the room. The force of its spirit still drifts like an odor throughout the house.

The power of that room, I have thought since, is very like the power of racism as status quo: it is deep, angry, eradicated from view, but strong enough to make everyone who enters the room walk around the bed that isn't there, avoiding the phantom as they did the substance, for fear of bodily harm. They do not even know they are avoiding; they defer to the unseen shapes of things with subtle responsiveness, guided by an impulsive awareness of nothingness, and the deep knowledge and denial of witchcraft at work.

The phantom room is to me symbolic of the emptiness of formal equal opportunity, particularly as propounded by President Reagan, the Reagan Civil Rights Commission and the Reagan Supreme Court. Blindly formalized constructions of equal opportunity are the creation of a space that is filled in by a meandering stream of unguided hopes, dreams, fantasies, fears, recollections. They are the presence of the past in imaginary, imagistic form — the phantom-roomed exile of our longing.

It is thus that I strongly believe in the efficacy of programs and paradigms like affirmative action. Blacks are the objects of a constitutional omission which has been incorporated into a theory of neutrality. It is thus that omission is really a form of expression, as oxymoronic as that sounds: racial omission is a literal part of original intent; it is the fixed, reiterated prophecy of the Founding Fathers. It is thus that affirmative action is an affirmation; the affirmative act of hiring — or hearing — blacks is a recognition of individuality that re-places blacks as a social statistic, that is profoundly interconnective to the fate of blacks and whites either as sub-groups or as one group. In this sense, affirmative action is as mystical and beyond-the-self as an initiation ceremony. It is an act of verification and of vision. It is an act of social as well as professional responsibility.

The following morning I opened the local newspaper, to find that the event of my speech had commanded two columns on the front page of the Metro section. I quote only the opening lines: "Affirmative action promotes prejudice by denying the status of women and blacks, instead of affirming them as its name suggests. So said New York City attorney Patricia Williams to an audience Wednesday."[4]

I clipped out the article and put it in my journal. In the margin there is a note to myself: eventually, it says, I should try to pull all these threads together into yet another law-review article. The problem, of course, will be that in the hierarchy of law-review citation, the article in the newspaper will have more authoritative weight about me, as a so-called "primary resource," than I will have; it will take precedence over my own citation of the unverifiable testimony of my speech.

I have used the Benetton's story a lot, in speaking engagements at various schools. I tell it whenever I am too tired to whip up an original speech from scratch. Here are some of the questions I have been asked in the wake of its telling:

Am I not privileging a racial perspective, by considering only the black point of view? Don't I have an obligation to include the "salesman's side" of the story?

Am I not putting the salesman on trial and finding him guilty of racism without giving him a chance to respond to or cross-examine me?

Am I not using the store window as a "metaphorical fence" against the potential of his explanation in order to represent my side as "authentic"?

How can I be sure I'm right?

What makes my experience the real black one anyway?

Isn't it possible that another black person would disagree with my experience? If so, doesn't that render my story too unempirical and subjective to pay any attention to?

Always a major objection is to my having put the poster on Benetton's window. As one law professor put it: "It's one thing to publish this in a law review, where no one can take it personally, but it's another thing altogether to put your own interpretation right out there, just like that, uncontested, I mean, with nothing to counter it."[5]

NOTES

1. "When 'By Appointment' Means Keep Out," *New York Times*, December 17, 1986, p. B1. Letter to the Editor from Michael Levin and Marguerita Levin, *New York Times*, January 11, 1987, p. E32.

2. *New York Times*, January 11, 1987, p. E32.

3. See generally *Blyew v. U.S.*, 80 U.S. 581 (1871), upholding a state's right to forbid blacks to testify against whites.

4. "Attorney Says Affirmative Action Denies Racism, Sexism," *Dominion Post*, (Morgantown, West Virginia), April 8, 1988, p. B1.

5. These questions put me on trial — an imaginary trial where it is I who have the burden of proof — and proof being nothing less than the testimony of the salesman actually confessing yes yes I am a racist. These questions question my own ability to know, to assess, to be objective. And of course, since anything that happens to me is inherently subjective, they take away my power to know what happens to me in the world. Others, by this standard, will always know better than I. And my insistence on recounting stories from my own perspective will be treated as presumption, slander, paranoid hallucination, or just plain lies.

   Recently I got an urgent call from Thomas Grey of Stanford Law School. He had used this piece in his jurisprudence class, and a rumor got started that the Benetton's story wasn't true, that I had made it up, that it was a fantasy, a lie that was probably the product of a diseased mind trying to make all white people feel guilty. At this point I realized it almost didn't make any difference whether I was telling the truth or not — that the greater issue I had to face was the overwhelming weight of a disbelief that goes beyond mere disinclination to believe and becomes active suppression of anything I might have to say. The greater problem is a powerfully oppressive mechanism for denial of black self-knowledge and expression. And this denial cannot be separated from the simultaneously pathological willingness to believe certain things about blacks — not to believe them, but things about them.

   When students in Grey's class believed and then claimed that I had made it all up, they put me in a position like that of Tawana Brawley. I mean that specifically: the social consequence of concluding that we are liars operates as a kind of public absolution of racism — the conclusion is not merely that we are troubled or that I am eccentric, but that we, as liars, are the norm. Therefore, the nonbelievers can believe, things of this sort really don't happen (even in the face of statistics to the contrary). Racism or rape is all a big fantasy concocted by troublesome minorities and women. It is interesting to recall the outcry in every national medium, from the *New York Post* to the *Times* to the major networks, in the wake of the Brawley case: who will ever again believe a black woman who cries rape by a white man?

Now shift the frame a bit, and imagine a white male facing a consensus that he lied. Would there be a difference? Consider Charles Stuart, for example, the white Bostonian who accused a black man of murdering his pregnant wife and whose brother later alleged that in fact the brothers had conspired to murder her. Most people and the media not only did not claim but actively resisted believing that Stuart represented any kind of "white male" norm. Instead he was written off as a troubled weirdo, a deviant — again even in the face of spousal-abuse statistics to the contrary. There was not a story I could find that carried on about "who will ever believe" the next white man who cries murder.

Acknowledgments

Meri Nana-Ama Danquah, "Life as an Alien" from *Half & Half: Writers on Growing Up Biracial and Bicultural* edited by Claudine C. O'Hearn. Copyright © 1998 by Meri Nana-Ama Danquah. Used by permission of Meri Nana-Ama Danquah. All rights reserved.

Brian Doyle, "The Greatest Nature Essay *Ever*" first appeared in the Nov/Dec 2008 issue of *Orion*. www.orionmagazine.com. Copyright © 2008 by Brian Doyle. Reprinted by permission of Brian Doyle.

Jenny Everett, "My Little Brother on Drugs" from *Popular Science*, April 2004. Copyright © 2011 Bonnier Corporation. 78537mo. Reprinted by permission of Wright's Reprints on behalf of *Popular Science*.

Anne Gisleson, "Your Exhausted Heart" from *The Oxford American*, August 2008. Copyright © 2008 by Anne Gisleson. Reprinted by permission of Anne Gisleson.

Meredith Hall, "Threshold" from *Without a Map*. Copyright © 2007 by Meredith Hall. Reprinted by permission of Beacon Press, Boston.

Courtney Moreno, "Fed to the Streets" first published in *L.A. Weekly* as "Help is on the Way." Copyright © 2009 by Courtney Moreno. Reprinted by permission of Courtney Moreno. Courtney Moreno worked as an EMT in Los Angeles for three years. She now lives in San Francisco, where she is earning an MFA and writing her first novel.

Tim O'Brien, "How to Tell a True War Story" from *The Things They Carried*. Copyright © 1990 by Tim O'Brien. Reprinted by permission of Houghton Mifflin Harcourt Publishing Company. All rights reserved.

Heather Rogers, "Sweet & Lowdown" from *Mother Jones* May/June 2010. Copyright © 2010 by Foundation for National Progress.

Heather Rogers and Dave Gilson, "Green on the Outside" from *Mother Jones* May/June 2010. Copyright © 2010 by Foundation for National Progress.

David Sedaris, "Ashes" from *Naked*. Copyright © 1997 by David Sedaris. By permission of Little, Brown and Company.

Zadie Smith, "Accidental Hero" from *Changing My Mind: Occasional Essays*. Copyright © 2009 Zadie Smith. Reprinted by permission of A P Watt on behalf of Zadie Smith.

Ellen Ullman, "Come In, CQ: The Body on the Wire" from *Wired Women: Gender and New Realities in Cyberspace*. Copyright © 1996 Lynn Cherny. Reprinted by permission of Seal Press, a member of the Perseus Books Group.